WORLD WAR I

A Turning Point in Modern History

BORZOI STUDIES IN HISTORY

CONSULTING EDITOR:

Eugene Rice, COLUMBIA UNIVERSITY

WORLD WAR I

A TURNING POINT IN MODERN HISTORY

Essays on the Significance of the War by

Gordon A. Craig, STANFORD UNIVERSITY

Carl J. Friedrich, HARVARD UNIVERSITY

Charles Hirschfeld, MICHIGAN STATE UNIVERSITY

Hans Kohn, EMERITUS, THE CITY UNIVERSITY OF NEW YORK

Edited with Introduction and Conclusion by

JACK J. ROTH

ROOSEVELT UNIVERSITY

ALFRED • A • KNOPF *New York*

THIS IS A BORZOI BOOK,
PUBLISHED BY ALFRED A. KNOPF, INC.

 Distributed by Random House, Inc. Published simultaneously in Toronto, Canada, by Random House of Canada Limited.

FIRST PRINTING

Library of Congress Catalog Card Number: 67–20629
Manufactured in the United States of America

Acknowledgments

I wish to thank Robert J. Ahrens, former Director of the Division of Continuing Education and Extension and now a Vice President of Roosevelt University, for his cooperation in making possible the four public lectures on which this collection of essays is based. The lecture series, presented in 1964 on the fiftieth anniversary of the outbreak of World War I, received the generous support of the Labor Education Division of the University, directed by Frank W. McCallister. Finally, I wish to express my gratitude to Don S. Kirschner and Georg G. Iggers for reading the final essay and to Roger Nash, the departmental graduate assistant, for his help in the preparation of the manuscript.

J. J. R.

CONTENTS

WORLD WAR I

A Turning Point in Modern History

I INTRODUCTION

Jack J. Roth

The half-century mark has recently been passed since the beginning of World War I. This collection of essays, however, has not been arranged to celebrate the occasion. One does not quite "celebrate" a disaster. Nor are we, necessarily, commemorating 1914—our purpose is not sentimental or nostalgic. We are not, in fact, concerned with the war, but with ourselves. What does the war mean to us today? Where do we stand—a half-century later—as a Western people, as Americans, with respect to the war?

Most historians today regard 1914 as a turning point in the history of the modern world, possibly on the same level of importance as 1789, the beginning of the French Revolution.

This view of the war's significance, however, is based on a fifty-year perspective—there have been other perspectives. Sir Edward Grey, the British Foreign Minister in 1914, was one of the few statesmen who had a foreboding of the darkness that was settling over the continent; but he was the exception—the number of statesmen who in 1914 foresaw the length, the ferocity, or the consequences of the war was small. Even the war years were marked by an extraordinary myopia. Apart from the more scurrilous forms of propaganda, most statesmen and peoples saw in the war primarily the fulfillment of their national aspirations. Others may have had a broader vision, but it was distorted by wishful thinking. Wilson, for example, saw in the war an end to international anarchy, a war that would end all wars. Lenin saw the war as the final stage of imperialism soon to open the gates to world revolution.

When the carnage ended, it was still possible in 1919, whatever the revulsion toward the war's destructiveness, for many to regard the outcome as consonant with the mainstream of nineteenth-century developments. After all, the war had resulted in the collapse of four autocratic empires—Russian, Turkish, Austrian, and German—and the freedom of a host of nationalities. Moreover, the new republics quickly provided themselves with democratic-sounding constitutions.

But to the postwar generation—the generation that saw the triumph of Bolshevism in Russia, the domestic chaos of the early twenties, and then the ravages of the Great Depression and the international chaos of the thirties, culminating in a second war in 1939—World War I was *the* great catastrophe that dominated their epoch. Those who knew the prewar world now looked back on the days before 1914 as a "Golden Age." What Talleyrand had said of 1789 was now said of 1914: those who were not alive before 1914 would never know how sweet life could be.

With the coming of the second war, the first seemed somehow less important, less spectacular—but not for long; since 1945 scholars have increasingly viewed World War I as decisive in modern history. It took a second world war to make the meaning of the first reasonably clear. It was the first war that fundamentally altered not only the character of European society, but Europe's relation to the rest of the world; it was the first war that made impossible the reconstruction of Europe and the restoration of her place in the world on a pre-1914 basis.

We have, of course, no assurance that our view of World War I is necessarily final. It probably is not. Every generation views the past, at least in part, in the light of its own experience, and our views are likely to appear outmoded to later generations. Moreover, we may be exaggerating the break with the past which 1914 has come to represent. In history, some would say, continuity and discontinuity are always intermingled—there are no "real" breaks. And in fact, much of what became characteristic of the postwar world was already in evidence, in one form or another, in the prewar years.

In what sense, then, however provisional, can the war be considered a "turning point"? Somewhere, and probably before 1914, Europe went off its nineteenth-century course. World War I, as well as the Bolshevik Revolution, the Great Depression, the totalitarianism of the thirties, and World War II may all have a vaguely common origin. We are living, possibly, in the midst of a huge convulsion in the affairs of men and the end is not yet.

Nevertheless, World War I possibly played a unique role in this convulsion—it may have "stacked the cards for the future." The war was in many ways without precedent: never had so many nations been involved; never had a war absorbed so much of the resources of the combatants or left them so exhausted; and never had the slaughter been of such magnitude or so senseless. In the Battle of Verdun, for example, casualties on both sides numbered over 750,000; at the Somme it was over 1,200,000 and the battle lines hardly changed. One out of every two French males who were between the ages of twenty and thirty-two in 1914 was killed during the war. If Europeans could accept casualties on such a scale, they could accept almost anything in the way of slaughter. The greatest tragedy of our time—its monstrous violence—begins in the trenches of World War I. Verdun and the Somme opened the way to Auschwitz and Hiroshima. The war, in any case, by virtue of its intensity, destruction, and duration served to "select out," to "favor," certain of the prewar tendencies; and while these persisted into the postwar era with renewed vigor, other tendencies were weakened or excluded.

In the essays which follow the topics are to be regarded as areas within which the authors are free to consider whatever they wish and in any manner they wish. The first three essays, however, are intended to have an essentially European, and the fourth an American, focal point. The intent of the Conclusion is to fill in gaps and to present a comprehensive view of the war's significance.

2 THE REVOLUTION IN WAR AND DIPLOMACY

Gordon A. Craig

A commemoration of the outbreak of the First World War cannot but be a melancholy affair. Few wars in history are capable of arousing such poignancy as this tragic conflict, perhaps because we have so much testimony to the mood of enthusiasm and hope and idealism with which it was entered into, and so many staggering statistics about the losses of those who shared those feelings. In 1939 soldiers went off to the front soberly, fatalistically, stoically, sometimes cynically: they had an awareness of what lay ahead. The recruits of 1914 rushed into conflict as if it were a feast or a frolic—"War is like Christmas!" said one young German with delight as he received his uniform and side arms—or they embraced it as a vital experience that would change and improve the world. Rupert Brooke sang:

Now, God be thanked Who has matched us with His
    hour,
And caught our youth, and wakened us from sleeping,
With hand made sure, clear eye, and sharpened power,
To turn, as swimmers into cleanness leaping,

Glad from a world grown old and cold and weary,[1] . . .

The same note was struck by young poets in other countries. In Germany, for instance, Bruno Frank wrote ecstatically:

> Rejoice, friends! that we are alive
> And that we're young and vigorous.
> Never has there been a year like this,
> And never has youth been so blessed.
>
> For we can stand and we can march
> Where the morning dawns and the evening sinks.
> The greatest of all epochs
> Puts its mark upon our young hearts.
>
> . . .
>
> And no matter what may befall any one of us
> He shall have seen this proud year.[2]

How brutally those fine hopes were disappointed we all know. The war that these young men expected never materialized. Instead, they had to experience what one of the characters in F. Scott Fitzgerald's novel, *Tender Is the Night,* described to some friends as they made a visit to the Somme valley after the war. "See that little stream," he said. "We could walk to it in two minutes. It took the British a whole month to walk to it—a whole empire walking very slowly, dying in front and pushing forward behind. And another empire walked very slowly backward a few inches a day, leaving the dead like a million bloody rugs." [3] Among those dead were many of the young

[1] "Peace," *The Collected Poems of Rupert Brooke* (1927), with an introduction by George Edward Woodberry and a biographical note by Margaret Lavington (New York, 1927), p. 111. Reprinted by permission of Dodd, Mead & Company, Inc. Copyright, 1915, by Dodd, Mead & Company; Copyright, 1943, by Edward Marsh.

[2] Bruno Frank, "1914," in Ludwig Reiners, ed., *Das ewige Brunnen* (Munich, 1955), p. 440; the translation is Professor Craig's. [Editor's note.]

[3] F. Scott Fitzgerald, *Tender Is the Night: A Romance,* with the author's final revisions (New York, 1948), p. 117.

idealists of 1914, whose vigor and intelligence might have helped change the world in many useful ways if they had been allowed to survive. In the Great War of 1914–18 the good died young and quickly. Alfred Duff Cooper tells us in his memoirs how he sat in the Foreign Office in London during the first year of the war and learned in despair of the death, one after another, of all of his closest Oxford friends. In her study of the Marne campaign, Barbara Tuchman tells the story of a young Frenchman who, because of illness, was unable to report to his unit for duty in August, 1914. As a result he was the only one from his *lycée* class of twenty-seven boys who was still alive by Christmas. It is stories like these, and their implications of dreadful waste, that make any commemoration of the Great War a somber and dispiriting business.

Even so, it is important that we do not avoid it. Before it was over, the war had wrought changes in almost every aspect of Western society—its structure, its institutions, its values—and it is possible that, if we look at those changes with the benefit of fifty years of hindsight, we may succeed in throwing a little light upon some of our present perplexities. These pages will attempt to deal with the effects of the 1914 conflict on two of the most important institutions of the Western world—war itself and diplomacy.

It is appropriate that these two be considered together, for they belong together. Classically, diplomacy was—in Sir Ernest Satow's definition—the process of employing tact and intelligence in the adjustment of the relations and the interests of independent states, and war was the means used for the same purpose when tact and intelligence failed. As the great German military theorist Clausewitz once explained, war was not an independent and self-sufficient agency, but merely a continuation of policy by other means. It was an instrument of statecraft, its ends and even its means determined by the requirements of policy, and its results defined and legalized by diplomatic negotiation.

The greatest statesmen of the nineteenth century understood this intimate relationship. At the time of Prussia's mobilization against France in July, 1870, for example, Bismarck read and underscored the phrase "Blessed are the peacemakers!" on his devotional wall calendar. This has sometimes been taken as a proof of the chancellor's essential cynicism; it might more properly be interpreted as a sign of determination on his part that the impending war would be kept within its political bounds and would be ended by diplomatic means as quickly as was expedient, once the state's political objectives had been secured. This kind of politico-military coordination was not always easy to achieve, and Bismarck himself had serious difficulties with the Prussian Chief of Staff during the last phase of the French war. But even so, despite the friction that occurred in concrete cases, there was, until 1914, fairly general agreement that the tasks of the soldier and the statesman (or diplomat) were complementary.

Perhaps the most fateful change effected by the First World War was the destruction of this relationship. Warfare was revolutionized in a way that made it increasingly difficult for civilian authorities to control. Simultaneously, the expanding violence of the conflict smashed the very framework of traditional diplomacy and released forces which, in the subsequent period, militated against the kind of consensus necessary to effective international collaboration and undermined the authority and prestige of professional diplomats in their own countries.

I

When we talk of the revolution that has taken place in warfare in our time, we think first of the frightening ways in which science and technology have enhanced its potential for destruction. This process, which culminated (or perhaps merely reached its penultimate stage of dreadfulness) in the Second World War, began during the first, and did so with a suddenness that startled the soldiers themselves. After one of the first British attacks in Flanders, a young subaltern said to Lieutenant General Sir Douglas Haig, "Sorry, sir. We didn't know it would be like that. We'll do better next time." The remark was prompted by the ghastly experience of learning for the first time what the combination of well-placed machine guns and barbed wire could do to massed attacks across an open field. Similar excuses must have been made on other occasions by regular officers of the armed forces—by Austrian commanders on the Drina and Galician fronts in 1914, for example, or by Russian officers on the Gorlice-Tarnow line in 1915—for those who had made a career of soldiering before 1914 always seemed to be more surprised than the non-professionals by the forms their vocation took during the First World War. Conventional assumptions about strategy and tactics were repeatedly shattered by the appearance of new weapons, or combinations of weapons, or techniques of combat. Neither the machine gun nor the use of wire was new in 1914, but their combination in articulated defensive systems and scientifically devised patterns of fire was new enough to have escaped the attention of those who made war plans, and this had a decisive effect upon the tactics of the war. Nor was this combination the only innovation. Others were the Big Bertha gun, the use of the submarine on a massive scale, the employment of smoke and poison gas to screen infantry attacks, the use of manned aircraft for reconnaissance, for anti-troop and anti-air combat, and for the bombing of installations, and the introduction of the tank. And this list is not exhaustive.

In the use of these weapons the armies of 1914–1918

were not always expert, and the results were sometimes modest. Only about 1,400 Englishmen and 750 Germans lost their lives as a result of air raids between 1914 and 1918 (a far cry from the 75,358 homes and residential buildings totally destroyed and the 135,000 persons who were killed in fourteen hours of aerial bombardment of Dresden in 1945). Poison gas proved an unpredictable weapon that was likely to kill as many friends as foes; the tank was misused in its first appearance in the field and played no important role until the war was almost over. Even so, the new weapons had come to stay; as time passed, they would be improved, and eventually they would be superseded by far more effective ones. There were people in the period after 1918 who tried to pretend that this was not so, and who sought to block new expenditure on armor or new experimentation with air power; but these were people who failed to draw the proper conclusions from the first worldwide conflict.

In a technical sense, the First World War, as Hanson Baldwin has written, "provided a preview of the Pandora's box of evils that the linkage of science with industry in the service of war was to mean." [4] It started that *Technisierung* of war which engrosses so much of the energies and resources of modern nations, and makes the average citizen so apprehensive of "missile gaps" and "technological breakthroughs" and other presumed threats to his security that he is apt to give uncritical support to his nation's armed establishment.

Important as this change in the nature of warfare was, it was less revolutionary than another: the extent to which war now absorbed the full energies of the societies that engaged in it. The war of 1914 was the first total war in history, in the sense that very few people living in the belligerent countries were permitted to remain unaffected by

[4] Hanson W. Baldwin, *World War I: An Outline History* (New York, 1962), p. 159.

it during its course. This had not been true in the past. Even during the great wars against Napoleon many people could go on living as if the world were at peace. All of Jane Austen's characters did so; none of them ever mentions the campaigns on the continent at all. It is said that on the evening of the allied disaster at Austerlitz there was great excitement in London, caused not by the military defeat, but rather by a boxing match between two well-known champions. This kind of detachment, which was true also of the wars in Central Europe in the 1860s, was wholly impossible during World War I. This was, for one thing, the first war in which the distinction between soldier and civilian broke down, a development that was partly due to the expansion of warfare made possible by those technological innovations already mentioned. When dirigibles began to drop bombs over London and submarines began to sink merchant ships, war had invaded the civilian sphere and the battle line was everywhere.

But this relative universalizing of the possibility of death in battle was not the only thing that made war total. Even when the dirigibles did not come, the civilian was caught up in the war and all of his activities were geared to its requirements. Once it had been discovered, in the winter of 1914, that the war was not going to be over by Christmas, that it was not going to be a short war like those of 1866 and 1870, and that it was not going to be won by military means alone but by the effective mobilization of the total resources of the nation and its allies, every mature citizen became an active participant in the war effort. He was subjected to disciplines and deprivations similar to those binding on the soldiers at the front, restrictions upon his freedom which varied with the fortunes of war and the distance of his country from the theater of operations. The energy and morale of the civilian now became just as important a resource as the spirit and determination of the man in the trenches—

which, of course, is why the enemy tried to drop bombs on him or starve him into compliance with its will.

Moreover—and here we come to the most fateful aspect of these changes—precisely because war became so total and was so prolonged, it also became ideological, taking on a religious cast that had not characterized warfare in the West since the Thirty Years' War. Frontline soldiers could feel sympathy for fighting men on the other side who had to put up with the same dangers and miseries that they bore themselves; and, on holidays, they could even declare private armistices with them and exchange presents. Aviators, with a chivalry that belonged to older forms of war, were known to drop wreaths on the graves of enemy fliers or—as in the case of the German ace Richthofen, who was shot down behind French lines—to give them elaborate funerals. The civilian was not given to this kind of behavior. He could not look the enemy in the face and recognize him as another man; he knew only that it was "the enemy," an impersonal, generalized concept, that was depriving him of the pleasures of peace. As his own discomfort grew, his irritation hardened into a hatred that was often encouraged by government propagandists who believed that this was the best way of maintaining civilian morale. Before long, therefore, the enemy was considered to be capable of any enormity and, since this was true, any idea of compromise with him became intolerable. The foe must be beaten to his knees, no matter what this might cost in effort and blood; he must be made to surrender unconditionally; he must be punished with peace terms that would keep him in permanent subjection.

The result of this was that the cautionary precept of Clausewitz was ignored and that rational calculation of risk versus gain, of compromise through negotiation versus *guerre à outrance*, became virtually impossible for the belligerent governments. There were soldiers and statesmen during the First World War who understood the truth later expressed by Professor Herbert Butterfield, when he wrote, after the second world conflict:

> If you possess an international order, or if it is your desire to assert the existence or the authority of such an order, you are the party which must refrain from conceiving the ends of war as though you were fighting barbarian hordes entirely outside the system. . . . So long as an international order exists, or so long as we may desire one to exist, wars must come short of the last degree of irreconcilability and must retain some of the characteristics of a conflict between potential allies, some trace of the fact that they are quarrels between friends.[5]

Unfortunately, those who felt this way were few and ineffective. As the war expanded in scope and violence, the masses who had to bear its rigors closed their minds to reason and called for a war of extermination.

It is sometimes pointed out, as a proof of the power of special interest groups in the determination of Germany's wartime policy, that both Chancellor Theobald von Bethmann-Hollweg and Foreign Minister Richard von Kühlmann were forced out of office because they advocated a peace short of total victory. It is true that these officials were the victims of a military–big-business cabal that did not want a negotiated settlement, but it is surely worth noting that their dismissal elicited not the slightest evidence of any popular indignation over the treatment accorded them. Nor should it be forgotten that, when former Foreign Secretary Lord Lansdowne, sickened by the slaughter in the trenches, wrote a letter to the *Daily Telegraph* in November, 1917, in which he urged that a negotiated peace be arranged while there was still something of European civilization to save, he was viciously attacked by the Northcliffe and Rothermere press, denounced

[5] Herbert Butterfield, *Christianity, Diplomacy and War* (New York, n.d.), pp. 96–97.

by politicians who described his letter as "craven" and "inept," and—in the words of his biographer—subjected to "a flood of invective and an incredible mass of abusive correspondence which, though largely incoherent, was marked by a violence rare in English political life." [6]

In the First World War, popular passion was probably more responsible than governmental obtuseness, not only for the prolongation of the war to the point where the old framework of Europe was smashed beyond repair, but also for the worst of the mistakes made at the peace conference as well. It is easy to understand why Jan Smuts of South Africa, watching war-induced hatreds prevail over reason at Paris, should have been moved to tell his friend John Maynard Keynes the story of the old Griqua chief, who, in perilous times, prayed: "Lord, save Thy people. Lord, we are lost unless Thou savest us. Lord, this is no work for children. It is not enough this time to send Thy son. Lord, Thou must come Thyself." [7]

As a result of the First World War, therefore, the art of warfare had been revolutionized by technological innovation, extended in scope, and given a pseudo-religious cast—and for all of these reasons it had become more dangerous, more destructive, and much more difficult to get back under control once it had been loosed.

II

The changes wrought by the war in diplomacy were equally profound and were rooted in the tendency of warfare to assume its absolute and most unrestrained forms by 1917 and 1918.

In the first place, as has already been indicated, the

[6] Lord Newton, *Lord Lansdowne: A Biography* (London, 1929), pp. 468–69.

[7] W. K. Hancock, *Smuts: The Sanguine Years, 1870–1919* (Cambridge, 1962), p. 521.

very context within which diplomats had operated in the past was altered out of recognition by the prolongation of the war. The nineteenth-century diplomatic system—Europe-centered and dominated by five self-confident and, for the most part, monarchical powers—dissolved in a holocaust unparalleled in history. The Habsburgs, the Hohenzollerns, and the Romanovs now left the stage of history, and out of their empires the peace-makers in Paris fashioned new states that entered the diplomatic community without either tradition or experience to guide them. The war also loosened the ties of empire, inspiring the British dominions to demand a stronger voice in the determination of imperial policy and arousing a desire for full sovereignty and independence in foreign affairs among the dependencies and protectorates of all colonial powers. Even during the course of the war, it had become apparent—with the intervention of Japan and the United States—that Mazzini's description of Europe as the lever that moved the world was no longer a true one, and that the course of world affairs could no longer be determined by congresses or ambassadorial conferences like those of Berlin and Algeciras. With the sharp increase in the number of geographically diverse states participating in world affairs—a tendency accelerated by the Second World War—new forms of diplomatic organization had to be found; the League of Nations was only the first of the attempts made since 1919 to cope with this problem.

The expansion of the diplomatic community was not the only change. Equally disturbing in its effects was the breakdown of intellectual homogeneity of the diplomatic system. Before 1914, the states which were active in international affairs were in general agreement about basic things. As Charles Burton Marshall has written:

> Their regimes drew on a generally common fund of history. The frame of discourse among them was unified

> to a degree permitting any government participating significantly in world affairs to be confident of having its utterances understood by others in the sense intended. None was a revolutionary power. Ideologies were "a minor theme" through most of the period. . . . The basis of general order was not at issue. A common notion of legitimacy prevailed.[8]

After 1918, all that was changed. The nations no longer accepted the same norms of international behavior, and it was often true that their representatives used the same words in ways quite different from their colleagues from other lands.

The fact that the war ended, on one hand, in revolution and, on the other, with a punitive peace settlement made this almost inevitable. In the first flush of their victory, the new regime in Russia, for example, made their rejection of all of the principles of the old diplomacy explicit, and Lenin and Trotsky earnestly attempted to abolish what they considered a wicked bourgeois institution that was wholly inappropriate for a proletarian state. When this attempt failed and they were forced in self-defense to cultivate contacts with other powers through traditional channels, and even to seek admittance to organizations like the League of Nations, they practiced diplomacy in what they considered to be the true bourgeois spirit—with as much disingenuousness, duplicity, and cynicism as they could get away with. Secretary of State Bainbridge Colby wrote indignantly in 1920 that the government of the United States had become convinced, against its will, that "the existing regime in Russia is based upon the negation of every principle of honor and good faith, and every usage and convention, underlying the whole structure of international law; the negation, in short, of every principle upon which it is possible to base

[8] Charles Burton Marshall, "The Golden Age in Perspective," *Journal of International Affairs*, XVII, 1 (1963), 11.

harmonious and trustful relations, whether of nations or of individuals." How could there be any common ground, he asked, upon which the Western powers could stand with a government whose conceptions of international relations were so entirely alien to their own? [9] This was a question that must often have been in the minds of diplomats whose governments could not, like the United States government, simply ignore the Soviet Union and who, therefore, had to go on trying to adjust their traditional concepts of diplomatic practice to Soviet wrecking tactics.

Nor did they have to concern themselves only with Lenin and his successors. Governments that resented the treatment they had received at Paris were not disinclined to follow the Soviet example, and some of them found leaders whose virtuosity matched that of the men sent forth from the Kremlin. Mussolini built a career upon his discovery that a flagrant breach of custom sometimes elicited more consternation than effective resistance; and Hitler won his early successes by means of outrageous falsehoods that were accepted by Western statesmen schooled in the tradition that diplomats were gentlemen and gentlemen did not lie to each other. In a sense, the whole period between the two world wars was a *dialogue des sourds* between those governments attempting to construct a genuine comity of nations on the ruins left by the war and seeking new rules that would be accepted by all its members, and those revolutionary powers that preferred to recognize no rules at all or desired to retain the freedom to determine when they would obey rules and when they would break them.

The degeneration of accepted standards of international intercourse and the confusion of the intellectual atmosphere in which diplomacy had to be conducted was further increased by the fact that the newly created or re-

[9] U.S. Department of State, *Foreign Relations of the United States* (Washington, D.C., 1920), Vol. III, 460 ff.

cently liberated nations were also likely to show a disinclination to accept traditional restraints. Their late arrival on the scene and their relative lack of status was often in itself a goad to defiance of the restrictions that a genuine community of nations requires; and in some cases resentments inherited from a colonial past inspired a rejection of legal arrangements, diplomatic principles, or methods of procedure simply because they were Western in origin or character. The behavior of the new nations—regarded from the standpoint of self-interest—was often illogical and self-defeating; but their leaders ignored this in their gratification over the confusion they proved capable of creating, and contributed powerfully to the complexities and the failures of communication of the new diplomacy.

Finally, it should be noted that in those countries having the greatest interest in maintaining public law and creating an effective international system after 1919, the ability of professional diplomats to cope with the problems caused by the war was seriously diminished by the loss of their former prestige and public support. In Great Britain and the United States in particular, it was widely believed that the diplomats had caused the war, because they had been the authors of what Woodrow Wilson called that "concatenation of alliances and treaties, [that] complicated network of intrigue and espionage which unerringly caught the entire family in its meshes." [10] As if intent on sharing Lenin's prejudices, politicians in both countries demanded that foreign policy be removed from the hands of the professionals and turned over to the people and were roundly applauded for doing so. There was little objection (except among officials of the Foreign Office and the State Department) when heads of state began to use persons with no special qualification in foreign affairs as

[10] Wilson on October 16, 1916, quoted in Bernadotte Schmitt, *Triple Alliance and Triple Entente* (New York, 1931), p. 1.

their diplomatic advisers, or to send politicians and businessmen abroad as envoys extraordinary in time of crisis, or even to go to foreign capitals themselves and to supersede their own ambassadors in negotiations.

George F. Kennan has written that summit diplomacy, a method of negotiation that has brought much imprecision and many unreasonable expectations into international intercourse since 1945, had its start during the Paris Peace Conference of 1919, where the Council of Four was a permanent summit conference in which heads of state, often without the assistance of professional diplomatic aides, sought to plaster loose formulae over intractable problems. Despite indifferent success at Paris, the experiment was carried further by the statesmen of the interwar period, the British being particularly prone to what came to be called "open diplomacy." Lloyd George, Ramsay MacDonald, and Neville Chamberlain all found it impossible to delegate the execution of policy and the delicate tasks of negotiation to professionals, of whom, indeed, they had an opinion bordering on contempt, and whose methods—the time-tested procedures of negotiation on the basis of written documents—they considered ill-suited to the conditions of the new age.

These tendencies, which had unfortunate results in British practice, were not confined to Britain. In France, when Briand and Laval were prime ministers, the Foreign Office was less than perfectly informed of the nature of their conversations with, and the extent of their commitments to, foreign statesmen like Stresemann and Mussolini. Nor would anyone deny that the distrust of professional diplomacy inspired by the First World War caused dislocation, imprecision, and confusion in the administration of foreign affairs in the United States. Wilson was not alone in his distrust of the techniques of the old diplomacy. The history of the London Economic Conference of 1933 and the elaborate methods employed subsequently by Franklin

Roosevelt to by-pass the State Department (methods commented upon most recently in the memoirs of Robert Murphy) were in full accord with the kind of pattern set by the Council of Four in 1919 and Lloyd George's personal diplomacy in the years that followed.

III

In the middle of the nineteenth century, Sir Robert Peel defined diplomacy as the great machine whose primary purpose was the preservation of peace. The revolutionary impact of the First World War upon the size and homogeneity of the diplomatic community and upon the nature of diplomatic practice was admirably designed to make the fulfillment of that purpose impossible and to release once more the expanding energies of war upon the world. How could the newer and smaller powers learn to cultivate restraint, responsibility, and recognition of collective values when older and stronger powers so conspicuously lacked those qualities? How could the *velléités* of Ramsay MacDonald or the arrogant amateurishness of Neville Chamberlain cope with the brutal forthrightness and lack of scruple of Mussolini or the deliberate obstructionism of the Soviet Union? Or, for that matter, with the ambitions of Adolf Hitler, who regarded diplomacy not as a machine for peace but as a means of preparing the way for the destructive war after which he lusted?

The Second World War was, to a very large degree, the direct result of the revolution in diplomacy that had been set in motion in the years between 1914 and 1918. At the same time, the second global conflict demonstrated that the technological and psychological changes affecting warfare in 1914 could be raised to new and frightening dimensions. The war that began with Stukas diving on Warsaw ended with the mushroom clouds over Hiroshima and Nagasaki, and, in the interval, any shadow of a line between soldier and civilian disappeared forever. The war became total to an extent that could not be exceeded; and it was fought with unimaginable bitterness to a point beyond all reason, until the destruction of the last vestiges of the system so badly shaken a quarter of a century before had been completed and the world had been handed over to the uncertainties of the Cold War.

The very employment of this term was an indication that war was threatening to become not only total but permanent, and that the passions that made men demand unconditional surrender in wartime were now affecting their minds as they thought about foreign policy in general. There were many occasions after the end of the Second World War when it appeared as if the democracies had won the war only to succumb to the views of diplomacy that had been professed by the totalitarian states. The whole atmosphere of international relations was impregnated with the smell of combat; and in the two great power centers of Washington and Moscow, the principal activity of diplomats seemed to be devoted to winning allies for some future, yet undisclosed, showdown. The idea of a compromise with the other side, of a *modus vivendi* that might stave off such a confrontation, seemed anathema to many people in the democracies; and Senator Joseph McCarthy found wide support when he conducted an investigation that soon became a persecution of supposedly unenthusiastic Cold Warriors in the diplomatic establishment. From being an instrument of policy, war seemed on the point of becoming its determinant.

And yet the very completeness of the technological revolution in warfare prevented these tendencies from reaching what might have seemed to be their logical conclusion. If, in a democratic age, where every man has a vital stake in foreign policy, war betrayed what Clausewitz once called a fatal thrust toward the absolute, it never quite got there. A sign that second thoughts might be asserting themselves was the fact that the Korean War was kept within bounds and restricted to the objectives that had been originally set for it, despite much violent talk about appeasement and about this being the only war the United States had ever lost. And in the subsequent period, diplomacy began to recover from the discredit that had been attached to it during the First World War and at periodic intervals thereafter, notably in the McCarthy episode. In the face of a clear possibility of a *dénouement* to the human drama like that portrayed in the film *Dr. Strangelove*, there grew a new appreciation of the uses of, and indeed a beginning of experimentation with new dimensions of, diplomacy.

In this last connection, we may revert to our starting point and recall the young idealists who dashed off to the front in 1914 with their hearts full of high resolve and their minds bent on that better world which would, they were sure, be the result of their sacrifice. It may be, as Professor Hermann Heimpel of the University of Cologne suggested in a recent address, that the present generation has rejected the notion that the highest good is to die for one's country and has substituted for this the ideal of living effectively for it instead. It may be that institutions like the Peace Corps—which has aroused so much interest and enthusiasm on American college campuses—may reveal new ways to achieve this ideal. In any event, it is permissible to hope that those members of the present generation who feel impelled, like Brooke's young men of 1914,

> With hand made sure, clear eye, and sharpened power,
> To turn, as swimmers into cleanness leaping, . . .

will turn, with all the idealism that is in them, to such works of mind and hand as may prevent the double revolution of war and diplomacy, to which these pages have been devoted, from reaching a fatal issue.

3 THE CRISIS IN EUROPEAN THOUGHT AND CULTURE

Hans Kohn

The war of 1914, rightly called the First World War, was the starting point of the first worldwide revolution. It originated in Europe but encompassed all of mankind within less than half a century. This revolution was universal not only in space; it was all-inclusive in content, everywhere changing thought and cultural trends, political ideas, and social structures.

Yet in 1914 the political and social life of Europe and the other continents seemed established on firm and apparently unshakable foundations. Europe led the globe in all fields of human endeavor. The great European powers and even some smaller countries, like the Netherlands or Belgium, were masters of vast stretches of the earth. Above all, Asia and Africa were almost in their entirety under direct or indirect European control. In the Western hemisphere, the United States exercised dominant control: it had secured by typically imperialist methods the building and the ownership "in perpetuity" of the Panama Canal; its armed forces intervened in Mexico and in other American republics. In Europe, the old social structures and traditional pomp of monarchy with its feudal background prevailed almost everywhere. Barbara Tuchman started her recent book *The Guns of August* with a brilliant description of the royalty of all countries assembled at the funeral of King Edward VII in 1910. Nobody then foresaw that this was the last display of the magic of monarchy. What has since been called *la belle époque* ended with this sunset of semifeudal aristocratic Europe. In the half-century since 1914, egalitarian forces have begun to assert themselves around the globe.

Representative of the old Europe were the conservative and military monarchies of Germany, Austria-Hungary, and Russia. Their rulers always appeared in public in military dress, surrounded by aides in equally resplendent uniforms. The monarchs of these three lands had been signers of the Holy Alliance in 1815, at the end of the long wars of the French Revolution and of Napoleon. The Holy Alliance was devised to protect Europe, above all Central and Eastern Europe, from the penetration of democracy, of constitutionalism, nationalism, and republicanism. Now, one century later, with the outbreak of World War I, the last traces of the Holy Alliance disappeared, and as a result of a war for which these empires bore the chief responsibility, the three dynasties fell. In 1910 they all, especially the Hohenzollern in Germany, seemed firmly established; no one would have then believed that by 1920 their thrones would be vacant and that by 1960 no one would dream of their restoration. The royal houses of Spain and Italy and of many Balkan kingdoms followed in the next decades. Only the democratic monarchies of northwestern Europe survived, and did so because they had long given up the struggle against democracy and popular sovereignty.

The political and social order that emerged in 1918 from the ordeal of war roughly corresponded to the demands of the European liberals of 1848 and even went beyond their aspirations. Republics replaced old-fashioned monarchies; the new constitutions stressed the sovereignty of the people; suffrage became general everywhere; women received the vote; labor legislation improved the condition of the working class; in many countries—where it would have been unthinkable before 1914—representatives of labor occupied the seats of power or entered as equal partners into coalition governments. The United States had not only helped to decide the outcome of the war; the Americanization of Europe began to undermine the hierarchical stratified European system. It did so less by the mechanization of life than by the spread of equality and social mobility in a way foreseen by Tocqueville.

The struggle between aristocracy and democracy, begun in the second half of the eighteenth century, seemed in the first half of the twentieth century to have been decided in favor of democracy. This victory profoundly changed the intellectual and social climate of Europe. Even the revolutionary movements opposed to equality and individual liberty that triumphed in Europe in the 1920s and 1930s were, with the exception of Generalissimo Franco's regime, not undertaken on behalf of the old ruling classes of the ancien régime. They were not movements of restoration, such as those of the Metternich era, dedicated to intellectual and social immobilism. They expressed the deeply disturbed feelings and aspirations of the lower middle classes in socially and politically retarded countries. These groups felt ill at ease and insecure in the new climate of liberty and rationality which the victory of the Western democracies, particularly the United States, promised to post-World War I Europe.

When we turn to the crisis in European thought and culture which emerged from the bitter struggle of more than four years, we must keep in mind the complexity and contradictory character of every historical epoch. New forces and attitudes emerge, but old attitudes continue to exercise their power over men's hearts and minds. And the old and the new may enter into many and highly varied combinations. Nevertheless, the end of World War I marked a definite turning point. No thinking man who lived through the two first decades of our century could fail to be aware of the crisis, though agreement regarding its nature might be difficult. Most people, of course, tried to live as if nothing fundamental had changed. They clung desperately to old and waning securities—the smugness and surface stability of the late-Victorian and Edwardian period. They tried to do so until the unprecedented economic depression of the 1930s and the rapid spread and easy victories of fascism shattered these illusions forever.

Yet warning voices were not lacking. At the end of the war, amid Western jubilation of victory and expectations of a return to "normalcy," a great French thinker and poet, Paul Valéry, observed in an address at Oxford that an extraordinary shudder had passed through the marrow of Europe. "We modern civilizations have learned to recognize that we are mortal like the others. We feel that a civilization is as fragile as a life."

With unusual perspicacity, then little heeded, he predicted that the transition from war to peace would be infinitely more dangerous and more obscure than the passage from peace to war: that all nations would be convulsed by it; that in a short while we might behold the spectacle of a strictly animal society, a perfect and final ant hill; and that Europe might lose her leadership and become what she was in reality, a little cape of the Asiatic continent. Three years later, in a lecture at Zurich, Valéry once more spoke of the "crisis of the mind" in the wake of the war. Today his pessimism and anxiety have become familiar, but in the fall of 1922 they sounded strange, and in the rising mood of optimism after 1924 (with Germany's economic recovery, America's prosperity, the

Locarno treaties, and the Kellogg pact) they were quickly forgotten:

> The storm has died away, and still we are restless, uneasy, as if the storm were about to break. Almost all the affairs of men remain in a terrible uncertainty. We think of what has disappeared, and we are almost destroyed by what has been destroyed; we do not know what will be born, and we fear the future, not without reason. We hope vaguely, we dread precisely; our fears are infinitely more precise than our hopes; we confess that the charm of life is behind us, abundance is behind us, but doubt and disorder are in us and with us. There is no thinking man, however shrewd or learned he may be, who can hope to dominate this anxiety, to escape from this impression of darkness, to measure the probable duration of this period when the vital relations of humanity are disturbed profoundly.
>
> One can say that all the fundamentals of our world have been affected by the war, or more exactly, by the circumstances of the war; something deeper has been worn away than the renewable parts of the machine. You know how greatly the general economic situation has been disturbed, and the polity of states, and the very life of the individual; you are familiar with the universal discomfort, hesitation, apprehension. But among all these injured things is the Mind. The Mind has indeed been cruelly wounded; its complaint is heard in the hearts of intellectual men; it passes a mournful judgment on itself. It doubts itself profoundly.[1]

In these words Valéry exposed the fundamental crisis of the twentieth century. Although Valéry belonged to victorious France, fears similar to this were even more strongly felt in Vienna, the capital that had lost, as a result of the war, much more than any great European city. There Hugo von Hofmannsthal, who was deeply shocked

[1] Paul Valéry, *Variety*, translated by Malcolm Cowley (New York, 1927), pp. 27–28. [Editor's note.]

by the collapse and break-up of his Austrian homeland, saw in the European situation of 1919 the opening of a grand new vista, "if one can bear to look it in the face." Apparently, he foresaw the possibility of new and daring adventures which he himself was much too civilized to follow. But soon a Central European youth marched forward (or backward?) over the "corpse" of a "decadent" civilization, and abandoning all the old norms and landmarks of civilized life, turned revolutionary in every field of thought and conduct.

I

The nineteenth century with its ideas of individual rights—attainable only in a moral climate of tolerance, compromise, and fair play—had its foundation in middle-class society with England as its model. Slowly, by the end of the century, such a middle class and its intelligentsia began to grow up throughout Europe, even in Spain, the Balkans, and Russia. Liberal thought penetrated fortresses of traditionalism and political underdevelopment. But outside the northwestern corner of Europe, where alone in Europe the liberal way of life was firmly rooted, the war's physical devastations, inflation, taxation, and confiscation took their toll of the economic foundations of the middle class and eroded the recently made gains of liberalism.

The economic destruction of the prewar social order was largely confined to Central and Eastern Europe. But the cruel wound inflicted on the European mind, of which Valéry spoke, was a general European phenomenon. The consolidated societies of the West could survive under its strain and preserve the liberal tradition of the late nineteenth century; the politically and socially less-developed societies of Central and Southern Europe—Italy, Germany, Spain, and the new countries of Central Eastern Europe—succumbed to the strain. Everywhere, though in varying degrees, the feeling of anxiety spread, and, perhaps as an antidote to it, a new emphasis on "living," on sex, a growing inclination to aggressiveness, and a search for individual security in complete subordination to collectivity and authority.

These phenomena were, of course, not entirely new. The stream of history flows, it does not start—the crisis in European thought and culture did not set in suddenly at the end of the war. The war itself, it may be said, resulted not only from decades of German aggression, from the general ineptitude of European diplomatic and military leadership, but also from a growing disarray of the European mind. The war failed to resolve those problems and, in fact, intensified and accelerated their development into the postwar era. All this was to lead, scarcely twenty years later, to the repetition of the First World War, but in a profoundly deepened atmosphere of intellectual and moral crisis. Compared with 1939, the years before 1914 appeared almost idyllic. But this was more apparent than real; the fermentation was already underway.

Romain Rolland had written in the 1903 introduction to his three *Heroic Biographies* that "old Europe" was oppressed by a "materialism without grandeur," and called for a new heroism. Rolland's "heroes" were great ethical creative minds of the past—Michelangelo, Beethoven, and Tolstoy. But these were not the heroes others craved. European youth still found the air suffocating and gave itself increasingly not to a self-disciplined effort of the mind, but to despair or to self-indulgence or to the glorification of mindless vitality and activity. In the last volume ("La Nouvelle Journée," 1912) of his great prewar novel *Jean-Christophe*, Rolland drew a picture of the new youth of Europe:

> In Europe a generation was arising, desirous rather of action than of understanding, hungry rather for happiness than for truth. It wished to live, to grasp life,

even at the cost of a lie. Lies of pride—all manner of pride; pride of nation, pride of caste, pride of religion, pride of culture and art—all were food to this generation, provided that they wore armor of steel, provided that they could be turned to sword and buckler, and that, sheltered by them, they could march on to victory. . . .

The new generation, robust and disciplined, was longing for combat, and, before its victory was won, had the attitude of mind of the conqueror. This generation was proud of its strength, its mighty chest, its vigorous senses so thirsting for delight, its wings like the wings of a bird of prey hovering over the plains, waiting to swoop down and try its talons. The children of the nation who had never seen war except in books had no difficulty in endowing it with beauty. They became aggressive. Weary of peace and ideas, they hymned the anvil of battle, on which, with bloody fists, action would one day new-forge the power of France. In reaction against the disgusting abuse of systems of ideas, they raised contempt of the idea to the level of a profession of faith. Blusteringly they exalted violent realism, immodest national egoism, trampling underfoot the rights of others and of other nations, when it served the turn of their country's greatness. They were not content to despise—they regarded the gentle dotards, the humanitarian thinkers of the preceding generation, as public malefactors.[2]

The "dehumanization" of art, to use a word coined by the Spanish writer José Ortega y Gasset, also began early in the century. In 1907, Pablo Picasso painted his "Les demoiselles d'Avignon" and in the same year Georges Braque introduced the cubist movement. Robert Delaunay, in 1914, painted his "Rythmes circulaires" and his "Disques simultanées" in which he combined a futurist dynamism and an analytical cubism. The French poet

[2] Romain Rolland, *Jean-Christophe* (Paris, 1926), Vol. X, pp. 201–2; the translation is Professor Kohn's. [Editor's note.]

Guillaume Apollinaire found the name "orphic"—an art which is non-representative, proceeding from "inner subject" rather than "external reality"—for the new style. The word "orphic," taken from ancient Greek mysteries, connoted the Dionysian and Titanic element in human life. Delaunay influenced some German and Russian painters in Munich who, in 1911, formed "The Blue Horseman Group." Wassily Kandinsky was to become its most distinguished exponent; others included August Macke and Franz Marc, who were both to die during the war. Arnold Schönberg in Vienna wrote in 1911 his "Sechs Kleine Klavierstücke," in which he first employed atonal harmony, though his twelve-tone technique was not fully employed until 1924 in his "Suite for Piano."

Even more important were certain currents of thought in opposition to the prevailing rational optimism and belief in progress. In 1900, Sigmund Freud published his *Interpretation of Dreams,* emphasizing the fundamental importance of man's subconscious and the all-pervading force of sexuality. Fillippo Tommaso Marinetti proclaimed in his "Futurist Manifesto" of 1909 the beauty and desirability of aggressiveness, danger, and war. Dynamism, the rejection of the past and the quest for a new vitality, became the mark of both the "true" art and the "real" life. Georges Sorel published his *Reflections on Violence* in 1908 and affirmed the creative role of violence and of social myths for history and for man's morality. Sir James Frazer drew attention in his *The Golden Bough* to archaic and erotic magic and folklore. As his work became better known, its influence coincided with the discovery of the esthetic appeal of primitive art. In Germany, where the disarray of the European mind was deepest (possibly because of the discrepancy between a highly advanced technology and a backward social order), the visionary pathos of the new expressionism was symptomatic of a rebellion against conventional ways of life and morality, of a demand for total renovation of the social and intellectual order.

II

Before World War I, however, this ferment was confined to very small circles. After the war it became general.

One of its chief qualities was "anxiety," a word used several times by Valéry in the passage quoted earlier. Old political and social certainties had been suddenly shaken; after four years of death and destruction, European mankind now found itself on the brink of an abyss. Victory and defeat had long hung in precarious balance. The horsemen of the Apocalypse had appeared not only over the battlefields, but had begun their bloody gallop across the vast snowfields of a Russia torn by revolution and civil war in the winter of 1917–18. The future seemed far less uncertain in the victorious West than in Central and Eastern Europe. But everywhere there reigned a general feeling of social and intellectual, economic and political insecurity. The past seemed dead. Who could say where the future might lead?

Thus *Angst*, anxiety or dread, dominated much of Europe. In Russia, however, the victorious Bolsheviks overcame it with the rational-optimistic certainty of the Marxian interpretation of history. The Leninist faith replaced the unheroic man of anxiety that we find in Boris Pasternak's *Dr. Zhivago* with an activist hero whose confidence in progress and in the blessings of a mechanized civilization exceeded even that of the bourgeois in the nineteenth century. But Germany discovered in its defeat and disarray a long-forgotten and practically unknown nineteenth-century Danish writer and theologian, Sören Kierkegaard, who had been obsessed by his view of man as a fearful creature, lonely and unprotected amid the dangers of life. At the end of the war Kierkegaard influenced two then-young men: Karl Barth, a parson in a small Swiss village who in 1919 published an exegesis of the *Epistle to the Romans*, and the philosopher Martin Heidegger, whose chief work *Being and Time* appeared in 1927. Both were among the most influential thinkers of postwar Germany. In Italy as well, there was profound malaise, but it took the form of frustration and anger rather than despair. Italy had been on the side of the victors, but the fruits of victory had matched neither Italy's enormous losses nor her inflated expectations.

With this disarray, felt above all in countries where the war had also revealed the fundamental weaknesses of an outmoded social order (as in Germany and Italy), went a craving for power, a cult of force, a desire to overcome anxiety and loneliness or frustration and anger in the excitement of combat and in the security of comradeship. A partly misinterpreted Nietzsche, whose will-to-power was more frequently invoked than his call to self-mastery, largely inspired among intellectuals a faith in the mission of supermen and super-races to establish their proud and hard dominion, to end the banality and mediocrity of "normal" life. Oswald Spengler simplified and vulgarized Nietzsche. Though Spengler was, as an intellectual, contemptuous of Hitler's mental primitivity, both nevertheless agreed that in history strength and success alone count, that "idle dreams" of universal truth and justice disappear in the dust heap of bookishness before the triumphant march of full-blooded he-men. Spengler, like Hitler, enthusiastically proclaimed the nihilism of all moral values. In the twenties, Spengler's *Der Untergang des Abendlandes* (*The Decline of the West*), as well as his later studies, confirmed many Germans in their contempt for Western rational values.

This adoration of violence reached its climax in fascism. Fascism did not originate in the thirties, but arose immediately out of the war. It appeared primarily in those countries where, as in Italy or Germany, many young men cherished their war experience as the most sublime moment of their lives, and where the horror of war (as expressed by Siegfried Sassoon or Wilfred Owen) had hardly any appeal among intellectuals. Fascism had a much greater following on the continent of Europe than rationalist Marxism or Russian communism. It appeared to be much more radical, for it rejected the whole modern development of Europe since the Enlightenment. It boasted of its strength; but in reality fascism was the extreme manifestation of intellectual disarray and fear—disarray about the validity of moral and rational values; fear of the "rise of the masses" which in 1930 Ortega y Gasset had delineated in his *Revolt of the Masses*.

This disarray led, on one hand, to utopian expectations of a total renovation of life out of the primary or primitive forces of the race, or out of a world purged of corruption and decay. The very chaos of the postwar era was to give birth to a new cosmos which would justify the sufferings of the war. The same distress produced, on the other hand, a deep pessimism, the discovery of the meaninglessness of life, of history, and of civilization. Many postwar youths in Central Europe and Russia felt for a brief moment the "transcendent power of creative joy" in revolution. But in most cases, joy turned to despair in a world of desolation and decaying values. The more sensitive were gripped, as Nietzsche had foreseen, by a fear of emptiness, by a feeling of the ground slipping beneath their feet.

The youth of Europe was in a state of feverish expectation. Two young and gifted French writers of the 1920s, Henry de Montherlant and André Malraux, did not regard the decade as an *après-guerre*, a postwar period, but as an *avant-guerre*, a prewar period. They were convinced that the prosperity and stability that followed 1924 was only temporary and that the great tragic course on which Europe had embarked would soon continue. Montherlant's early novels, *Les Olympiques* (1924) and *The Bullfighters* (1926), stressed the moral value of war (Montherlant had been wounded as an infantryman). But he rediscovered these values in athletic games and adventures, in bloody sports and bullfights, in everything which promised a life of great intensity, of spectacular danger. Life revels in its fundamentally absurd but exciting character: *jouer sa vie sur un jeu plus grand que soi*. This is the mood in Malraux's first novels, *Les Conquérants* (1928) and *La Condition Humaine* (1933), dealing with the Chinese revolution. But Malraux's concern was with the fundamental loneliness of man, with the comradeship, the betrayals, the borderline of existence between idealism and criminality familiar to us in Dostoevsky's *The Possessed*.

The immediate postwar period was a time in which excitement and sadness entered into a strange amalgam. Berthold Brecht, whose poetry will undoubtedly survive his plays, wrote of "dark times" and "terrible news." The vision of "terrible news" also haunted William Butler Yeats in 1919 in his famous poem, "The Second Coming":

> More anarchy is loosed upon the world,
> The blood-dimmed tide is loosed, and everywhere
> The Ceremony of innocence is drowned;
> The best lack all conviction, while the worst
> Are full of passionate intensity.
> Surely some revelation is at hand
> Surely the Second Coming is at hand.[3]

[3] William Butler Yeats, "The Second Coming," *The Collected Poems of W. B. Yeats* (New York, 1933), p. 215. Reprinted with permission of the Macmillan Company, Mr. M. B. Yeats, and Macmillian & Co. Ltd. Copyright, 1924, by The Macmillan Company. Renewed 1952 by Bertha Georgie Yeats. [Editor's note.]

The "Second Coming," however, was not that of the redeeming Christ, but of a rough and pitiless beast yet to be born. Yeats himself rejected all belief in progress and a rational future. He wrote in 1923 that the last war was neither the last nor was the world getting any better, and expressed his admiration for Mussolini.

The desolation of the year 1922, when Mussolini staged his March on Rome, was most memorably expressed in "The Waste Land" by the young American poet T. S. Eliot, who in 1914 had settled in London. The poem took its theme from the most famous Sibyl or prophetess of antiquity, that of Cumae near Naples, who was consulted by Aeneas before his descent into Hades and who sold her books of prophecy to Tarquinius Superbus, Rome's seventh king. Those Sybilline books predicting the future of Rome and the world were faithfully preserved in the capitol until its destruction by fire in 83 B.C. Asked by some boys what she wished, the Sibyl answered: "I wish to die utterly."

Sir Herbert Read has called "The Waste Land" "a mythological salad," and perhaps it is. Yet in its passages of retrospection and prophecy, it recalls Valéry's warning of the fragility and transitoriness of our civilization:

What is that sound high in the air
Murmur of maternal lamentation
Who are those hooded hordes swarming
Over endless plains, stumbling in cracked earth
Ringed by the flat horizon only
What is the city over the mountains
Cracks and reforms and bursts in the violent air
Falling towers
Jerusalem Athens Alexandria
Vienna London
Unreal[4]

[4] T. S. Eliot, "The Waste Land," *Collected Poems, 1909–1962* (New York, 1936), pp. 87–88. Copyright, 1936, by Harcourt, Brace & World, Inc.; Copyright, © 1963, 1964, by T. S. Eliot. Reprinted by permission of the publisher. [Editor's note.]

Shorter and even more impressive is the famous line:

London Bridge is falling down falling down falling down[5]

Eliot himself acknowledged his indebtedness to *The Golden Bough* which, he wrote, "has influenced our generation profoundly." The revival of myth as supreme expression of reality, the discovery of primitive or tribal art of which we have already spoken, became widespread in the immediate postwar period. The trend ran counter to the mainstream of Western development, for this primitivism had been overcome in antiquity by the Greeks in their love of living forms, in their love of the human and the natural. Now artists turned to conjuring up imaginary worlds, to rejecting reality in favor of experiment and new experiences. This quest for the prerational past of civilization corresponded to Carl Gustav Jung's search for the "archetypes of the collective unconscious" and the glorification of the primitive instincts and institutions of war and the warrior.

The gifted German author of the 1920s, Ernst Jünger, whose book *Stahlgewitter* (*Storms of Steel*), published in 1920, celebrated bloody battle as the highest of man's innermost experiences, supplied the spiritual support for General Ludendorff's doctrine of "total war," a fateful amalgam of tribal mythology and modern technology. Thomas Mann saw the problem of life from the standpoint of romantic myths—the fascination of death and disease, the proximity and inclination of the artist to morbidity, to adventure and to self-destruction. The hero of his novel *The Magic Mountain* (1924), Hans Castorp, "a simple young man" from a commercial middle-class background, after his seven years on the "magic mountain" of illness, recognized that: "What I had in me, as I quite clearly know, was that from long ago, even as a lad, I was familiar with illness and death. . . . for death, you know,

[5] *Ibid.*, p. 90. [Editor's note.]

is the principle of genius. . . . There are two paths to life: one is the regular one, direct, honest. The other is bad, it leads through death—that is the way of genius." [6] At the end, Castorp followed the regular and honest path —he joined the German army and died in the war.

Thomas Mann, like many of his contemporaries, was influenced by Nietzsche and Freud. However, the postwar age, dominated by this influence, disregarded essential aspects of their teachings. The visionary philosopher-poet and the therapeutic scientist, so different in their language, shared a tragic view of life and a humanistic stoic morality based on self-control and rationality. Both "unmasked" man, but in order to reveal his innermost aggressiveness and evil drives, and both praised self-mastery. In all men, Freud wrote in his *The Future of an Illusion* (1927), there were destructive antisocial and anticultural tendencies; for this reason, all civilized life rests on enforced renunciation. "Civilized man," Freud wrote in his *Civilization and Its Discontents* (1930), "has exchanged some part of his chances of happiness for a measure of security." [7] But Freud saw not only the security of the social order as dependent on self-restraint or the restraint imposed by society (the conquest of passion by reason); even cultural creativity was dependent on sublimated sexual energy transformed into "aim-inhibited *libido*." The rational human self, the *ego*, was the "rider" taming the "horse" of primeval passions, the *id*.

The widespread acceptance of psychoanalysis after the war—Freud influenced the surrealism of André Breton as much as the existentialism of Jean-Paul Sartre—did not cause the new sexual freedom which characterized the postwar era. Psychoanalysis offered a rationalization for this

[6] Thomas Mann, *The Magic Mountain*, translated by H. T. Lowe-Porter (New York, 1939), p. 752. [Editor's note.]

[7] Sigmund Freud, *Civilization and Its Discontents*, translated by James Strachey (New York, 1962), p. 92. [Editor's note.]

freedom, but licentiousness could find no support in either Freud's teaching or personal life. Probably all wars throughout history have increased sexual licentiousness. In previous epochs, including the pious Christian Middle Ages, "illicit" love was at least as common as after 1918 and prostitution at least as thriving. Sexual behavior after 1918 appeared "worse" because of the contrast with the Victorian age. That age and the great Victorians were held in low esteem in the 1920s. Lytton Strachey published his debunking biography of Queen Victoria in 1921 and the campaign against Victorian stuffiness and hypocrisy got quickly into full swing. John Maynard Keynes in his *The Economic Consequences of the Peace* (1919), an unfortunate by-product of this anti-Victorianism and anti-puritanism, treated Woodrow Wilson as the last Victorian and saw Wilson's aims as sham and hypocrisy. The new sexual freedom meant not a startling increase in "immorality," but an unprecedented open discussion of sexual problems, for which psychoanalysis supplied a rationale and a vocabulary.

The Oedipus complex, which in Freud's view was central to the antagonism and hostility of fathers and sons at all times and in all cultures, seemed to become especially characteristic of Western society in the twentieth century. Here we find for the first time the separation and conflict of generations as a general phenomenon. In the last decade before 1914, the German youth movement demanded freedom from traditional authority and the right to lead their own lives and to be guided by men of their own choice and generation. The early expressionist movement dramatized this conflict of generations by means of the theme of parricide. After the war, however, far-reaching structural changes in society contributed to the break-up of the traditional family: youth was impatient with tradition and attempted to establish its own patterns in amusement, art, and fashion, to which the trade and the advertising media began to cater. The authority of old age gave way to youthful self-assertion; the hostile tension so deeply felt in Freud's generation was, after the war, replaced by a mingling of generations on a new footing of equality. "Youth" changed from a biological stage in man's growth into an existential value in itself. In the Victorian age, men often looked older than they were; after 1918, elderly people wished to appear younger than they were.

Before 1914 free thinkers and socialists often rejected marriage as a religious or bourgeois institution, yet lived in fidelity with a "loyal companion for life." Though brought up as a Catholic in Ireland, James Joyce submitted to a civil ceremony after twenty-seven years of living with the same woman in order that his children, who had not been baptized, could inherit his property without difficulties. There was, before 1914, a rejection of outworn conventions and ritualist superstition, but not of the underlying ethos. Love preserved its fidelity and beauty. Joyce's *Ulysses* (1922) ends with Molly Bloom's famous monologue, based on the reunion of Ulysses and Penelope —a vision, in Richard Ellmann's interpretation, of the Garden of Eden. But, "there is no serpent in this garden, and without the serpent, there is no sin. The fall of man, instead of being bitter, is the sweetest memory we have. Molly and her husband live in a world where the devil had no place; and in the famous peroration of her monologue she says yes to her husband, to the flesh, and to all this neo-pagan world." [8]

In Joyce's neo-pagan world, the center of which is Homer's wisest, most human, and least martial hero, love is delight. After 1918 sex often assumed a more tortured character, a grim mixture of attraction and repulsion, a revival of the old order and darker gods of primitive times. Intellectuals rediscovered the Marquis de Sade. Their

[8] Richard Ellmann, *James Joyce* (New York, 1959), p. 388. [Editor's note.]

interest centered not so much in the long and repetitive narrative in his novels [with their ironic or provocative titles: *Justine ou les malheurs de la vertu* (1791) and *Les Histoires de Juliette ou les prospérités du vice* (1797)], but in his evaluation of criminal acts and sexual cruelty as "natural," as the highest affirmations of life. Sexual licentiousness was often not a gateway to a joyful Garden of Eden, but a triumph of chaos over law and order, a manifestation of the destructive urge in man. Sex and obscenity became a means of protest against a civilization and a social and political order which appeared to have led Europe into four years of unprecedented cruelty, destruction, and suffering.

This protest expressed itself during the war in Zurich in the birth of the Dadaist movement, a movement of young artists and intellectuals who found in neutral Switzerland a refuge from their wartorn homelands. Its founder was the artist Tristan Tzara, a Rumanian who later lived in France. Dadaism originated in a short-lived nightclub called Café Voltaire—African masks and Polynesian fetishes decorated the walls. Writers and artists in the movement wrote "manifestos" against civilization and society, noisy protests characterized by irrational phantasies and obscenities designed to shock the philistine and the "good citizen." Tzara's advice on how to write a poem was typical; he suggested cutting out words from a newspaper, putting them in a bag, shaking the bag, and then removing the words one by one. From a supposedly mature world which seemed to have gone mad and made no sense, refuge was sought in infantilism and provocative nonsense.

Dadaism lived on for a few years in Berlin, Cologne, and Paris and expressed itself in all art forms—in painting, sculpture, music, and poetry. Its violence was turned against a Europe which had fallen into chaos. But by 1922 the movement reached a dead end. Some of its leading participants, among them Tzara himself, started a new movement in Paris, surrealism, in which André Breton, a trained psychiatrist influenced by Freud, took the lead. Many contemporary artistic moods—those of the absurd or grotesque theatre, of black humor, of the bizarre, of the psychopathology of life and art, of despair in civilization—have their roots in surrealism. Surrealism tried to chart the newly discovered and unexplored continents of sensibility and the mind. In his *First Manifesto* (1924), Breton emphasized:

> . . . pure psychic automatism, by which it is intended to express the real process of thought, thought's dictation, in the absence of all control exercised by reason and outside all esthetic or moral preoccupations. Surrealism rests on the belief in the omnipotence of the dream and in the disinterested play of thought. . . . Breaking down the barriers both physical and psychical, between the conscious and the non-conscious, between the inner and the outer world, will create a super-reality, in which the real and the unreal, meditation and action meet and mingle and dominate the whole life.[9]

Surrealism attempted to recover the obscure subconscious, the pre-individual and prerational basis of human existence with its primitive and eternal myths and symbols. Under the influence of Arthur Rimbaud, surrealism saw in the artist, essentially, a magician.

Characteristic of the early postwar period was the surrealist faith in the omnipotence of desire, in the power of magic art to lay, among the ruins of the old world, the foundations of an earthly paradise. Nietzsche's influence and the example of Lenin's revolution were responsible for the amalgam of extreme scepticism with respect to the present and a burning faith in the future—the expectation of a forthcoming liberation of mankind, of a total revolution. Surrealism was an expression of the mood of the

[9] André Breton, *Manifeste du surréalisme* (Paris, 1924), p. 42; the translation is Professor Kohn's. [Editor's note.]

period. It was a revolutionary movement, *la Révolution d'abord et toujours*, and it went to absurd lengths in its desire "to systematize the intellectual and moral confusion and to contribute to the total discredit of the world of reality."

Originally non- or anti-Marxist, the surrealists began to cooperate with the Communists in protesting the colonial war against Mohammed Abd-el-Krim, an Arab leader of astounding energy and great ability who had challenged Spanish and French rule over Morocco and was defeated only by the combined efforts of the two European armies in 1926. Vincent Sheean in his *Personal History* (1935) has excellently portrayed the excitement caused by this war. This cooperation with the Communists, however, led in 1931 to a split in the surrealist movement. Some of its most gifted writers, Louis Aragon and Paul Eluard, for example, joined the Communist Party and accepted its discipline and order. Breton became a Trotskyite, but remained faithful to psychoanalysis and to total revolution. In his *Second Manifesto* (1930), he wrote: "Everything remains to be done; all means employed to ruin the ideas of family, fatherland, religion are good. The surrealist position in this respect is well known; one has to realize that it accepts no compromise." [10] Four years later, in his *Qu'est ce que surréalisme?* (1934) he reaffirmed, together with the independence of surrealism, its connection with the Leninist revolution (an attitude rather similar to that assumed twenty years later by Jean-Paul Sartre). But very different from the puritanism of Leninism was Breton's ecstatically proclaimed Dionysian cult of sex, announced in his *L'Amour fou* (1937):

> Love, unique love, carnal love, I adore your poisonous shadow. A day will come when man will adore you as his only master and will adore your secret perversions

[10] André Breton, *Second Manifeste du surréalisme* (Paris, 1930), p. 14. [Editor's note.]

by which you surround yourself. . . . It is necessary to exterminate the infamous Christian idea of sin. There never existed a forbidden fruit. Temptation alone is divine.[11]

This was written in the spirit of the 1920s, to which surrealism belonged. But before 1930, the *après-guerre*—with its intellectual distress and its ecstatic hopes, its life of frenzy, of flaming youth, of unbridled sex and its revolutionary violence—had come to an end. The euphoria that set in with the renewed prosperity after 1924, with the Locarno treaties, the Kellogg pact, and the weakening of Communist propaganda, seemed to promise a return to prewar stability and "normalcy."

But that was not to be: the economic depression, Hitler's rise to power, and the Spanish Civil War ended the short-lived recovery and initiated a chain of events which once again shook Europe to its foundations. The postwar period was transformed into a prewar period. But it had produced movements and trends which were to be carried over after World War II, though in a changed intellectual and moral climate, into the second postwar era.

[11] André Breton, *Poésie & autre* (Paris, 1960), p. 164. [Editor's note.]

4 THE RISE OF TOTALITARIAN DICTATORSHIP

Carl J. Friedrich

The speculations and researches about the origin of totalitarian dictatorship recurrently include the First World War as a seedbed of this novel form of government.[1] Yet there can be little doubt that the taproots of totalitarianism reach much further back. Its several ideologies, and more especially Marxism, did not at all envisage anything like the totalitarian dictatorships of the twentieth century. They nonetheless provided the utopian and chiliastic outlook which in its concrete application generated twentieth-century totalitarian dictatorship, first in the Soviet Union and, thereafter, in other countries. The First World War may, therefore, have had very little to do with the genesis of this new kind of autocracy, and the argument may be reduced to a simple *post hoc ergo propter hoc*. Or, alternatively, the First World War and totalitarianism may have their origins in the same source.[2]

[1] For a full exposition of Professor Friedrich's position, see Carl J. Friedrich and Zbigniew K. Brzezinski, *Totalitarian Dictatorship and Autocracy*, 2nd rev. ed. (New York, 1965). [Editor's note.]

[2] For an attempt to establish imperialism as the common source see Hannah Arendt, *The Origins of Totalitarianism*, 2nd enlarged ed. (New York, 1960). [Editor's note.]

One thing is certain: No one at the time of the start of the war had any inkling of totalitarianism nor, indeed, of what would be the consequences of that fateful conflict. There had been, before the war, many gloomy assessments of the future amid general optimism and shallow progressivism, but these failed to envisage the concrete form which the development would take. There can be little question that if those who made the crucial decisions, more especially the imperial governments of Austria-Hungary, Russia, Germany, and Britain, had had any prevision of what was to come, they would have exerted themselves a great deal more to avoid the outbreak of the war. Stimulated by wartime and postwar propaganda about "war guilt," historical scholarship has done and is doing a good deal to explore the responsibility for what happened in those weeks preceding August, 1914. A gradual broadening and deepening of scholarship related to the problem has occurred. The universal striving for maintaining or expanding imperial power has emerged as a crucial factor. There was active and passive responsibility—overreadiness to act, as well as failure to do so; both aggressive and defensive types of responsibility have come to share the blame. But, all in all, the origin of the war seems remote from our problem of the link between the war and the rise of totalitarianism.

One very simple argument might, on the other hand, link the concluding phase of the war to the emergence of totalitarianism by pointing to the decision of the German imperial government to permit Lenin to return to Russia after the fall of the tsarist regime with the purpose of overthrowing the Provisional Government, since the latter had decided to continue support of the Allied war effort. Or one could complicate the argument (and distribute the blame) by adding that the Allies had erred in demanding that the Provisional Government continue the war—the Allies should have urged stabilization of the regime and defense against the more radical elements. Surely, the cry for peace was the most effective weapon in Lenin's arsenal, and the desire to eliminate Russia from the war decisive in persuading the German imperial government to use Lenin. But such an argument, in any case, seems rather superficial, especially when not even Lenin, much less the Germans, had any idea of the menace of totalitarianism. To be sure, Lenin's theoretical and practical efforts to impose a rigidly autocratic and hierarchical pattern upon the Bolshevik party contained the seeds of coming developments. But they were, at the time, argued strictly in terms of the needs imposed on the movement by an autocratic and repressive tsarist regime which necessitated a corresponding discipline among those who were fighting for its overthrow.

I

The preceding argument raises the question of the nature of totalitarianism and totalitarian dictatorship. There has been a tendency in recent years to attribute the rise of totalitarianism to a variety of thinkers and movements, notably Marx, Hegel, Rousseau, and Hobbes. Indeed, some writers have gone even farther afield. Quite apart from the doubtful etiology which argues from thought to action in such naïve terms, the argument rests basically upon a misunderstanding of the nature of totalitarianism.

Hobbes and Rousseau were radical individualists and Rousseau, especially, an ardent humanitarian. Hegel was an old-fashioned constitutionalist whose key line of reasoning was that the history of man is the history of man's progressive realization of freedom. Marx, in turn, was an utopian democrat of the Rousseauist strand. He was a humanitarian who expected the revolution, after a brief period of "functional dictatorship" (an emergency regime), to lead to a classless society which would enjoy the benefits of self-administration without any further need of government—as late as 1921 Lenin still talked in terms of this "new kind of state." Marx was very proud of his realistic analysis of the economic situation of his time which was, indeed, even with all its shortcomings, a remarkable achievement. (What Marx would think of those of our contemporaries who apply his analysis to our very different economy is another matter.) But as often pointed out, the penetrating analysis of *Das Kapital* is not matched by any corresponding insight into what was to follow. Marx certainly did not think that anything even remotely resembling the Soviet Union, let alone Red China, would emerge from the overthrow of capitalism. Indeed, he spoke of the withering away of the state and of voluntary cooperation and mutual sharing. It is quite clear that the Marxist movement in virtually all countries in 1914 still entertained, although with somewhat lessened fervor, Marx's utopian and chiliastic hopes and expectations. A final condition of universal brotherhood was widely believed to be close at hand. Hence, it is unconvincing to link either the rise of totalitarianism—or indeed its nature—to the writings of those who contributed to the ideology of totalitarian movements, except in a very indirect way.

But once again the question of the nature of totalitarian dictatorship arises. There is a prevailing psychological interpretation which stresses the fact that this kind of government takes hold of man in his totality. It is undoubtedly something which totalitarian movements and governments seek to do, but by now the evidence is clear that they fail in this purpose, except with a small percentage of fanatical followers. Such "totalism," as it might more properly be called, is not entirely satisfactory as a characterization of totalitarian governments. Totalism has appeared recurrently in the theory and practice of politics; certain groups, such as primitive tribes, monasteries, and religious orders have been and continue to be radically totalist, but theirs is a far cry from totalitarianism. Plato's thought is also decidedly totalist, without being in any precise sense totalitarian, if by that term is meant a form of autocracy; for Plato was explicitly anti-autocratic and considered the autocracy of his time—tyranny—the worst form of government. We should seek, therefore, a more pragmatic characterization of totalitarian dictatorship that concentrates on what rulers and ruled actually do; we should talk about facts rather than moods, about structures and functions rather than their psychic concomitants.

There exist six basic traits of a totalitarian regime that distinguish it clearly from other types of autocracy and government.[3] First, there is a single mass party that claims the monopoly of political decisions. Second, we find an ideology of totalist scope; that is to say, it is based on a total criticism and rejection of the existing or preceding society and government and projects a utopian, chiliastic program for the future. The party is highly authoritarian and hierarchical in structure and, hence, typically headed by a single leader, the dictator; he frequently claims, especially in the initial stages, to be the authoritative interpreter of party doctrine. The dictatorially led party, taking full advantage of the means made available by modern technology, reinforces the government which implements its decisions by three kinds of monopoly: mass communications, effective weapons, and organizations. The third of these monopolies is especially in evidence in a centrally controlled and directed economy. The ideological position and the general control of the party is strength-

[3] For full development of this argument see Friedrich and Brzezinski, *op. cit.*, pp. 3–14. [Editor's note.]

ened by a sixth trait: a secret police apparatus which provides a near-total control of both the party and the subject population, giving rise to various kinds and degrees of terror—physical, economic, and psychological.

It is clear from the traits just sketched that one could describe a totalitarian dictatorship as an autocracy in the age of advanced technology, an autocracy resting upon a popular, mass-related legitimacy. That totalitarian dictatorship is clearly an autocracy requires emphasis; but it should not be confused with older forms of autocracy. In a sense, it is flattering to call a totalitarian dictatorship a despotism or absolutism or tyranny—these terms denote something much less formidable. The older types of autocracy were much less comprehensive in their oppressive control of persons and groups, and certainly never sought or exercised a monopoly of communications or organizations, or even of weapons. In fact, the possibility of armed rebellion typically served to restrain the older autocracies. But rebellion is impossible under totalitarian dictatorship, since the controls are such that an opposition cannot organize, let alone effectively arm and fight.

It is necessary to add to this contrast another—that between the totalitarian and the old-fashioned kind of military dictatorship of which the regimes of the two Napoleons in France are the outstanding illustrations. The latter is recurrent in Latin America and in other countries with unstable political conditions. The function of such dictatorships is conservative and at times restorative, although elements of a revolutionary transformation may be present, as in the case of the first Napoleon and Mustafa Kemal Ataturk. This type of regime, based on military control, is usually ideologically weak and inadequately legitimized. It has been proposed that these be called "functional" dictatorships. But the term functional is too broad for effectively characterizing this form of dictatorship, and "military" is adequate for distinguishing it from totalitarian regimes.

II

Once totalitarian dictatorship is thus understood, it is quite clear that no such regime arose or was foreshadowed by developments during the First World War.

The war itself was not a totalitarian enterprise. Even its most radical ideological thrust, epitomized in such Wilsonian slogans as "making the world safe for democracy" and "open covenants openly arrived at," was progressive rather than revolutionary in its approach toward existing society and the possibility of its reform. The war economies were not totalitarian, although in all the major countries governmental controls were expanded and planning extended, if not in fact innovated. Nor were the people engaged in the war in any sense totalitarian in mind and outlook. There were imperial designs, as previously indicated, but these mostly took the form of territorial expansion. German public opinion may have supported a "*Griff nach der Weltmacht*," [4] British and French opinion been ready to defend their empires, and American opinion eager to expand "democracy"; but these were goals in line with established traditions and prevailing views, not totalitarian and utopian.

And yet, the war cleared the ground for the rise of totalitarian dictatorship. Not only did it undermine the traditional order in Russia, Austria-Hungary, Germany, and Italy, and thereby create considerable *anomie*,[5] but it also

[4] The reference is to an impressive reassessment of the war's origins in Fritz Fischer, *Griff nach der Weltmacht* (Düsseldorf, 1962). [Editor's note.]

[5] The term was first introduced by the French sociologist Émile Durkheim in a celebrated study of suicide and defined as a social condition in which the hierarchy of values disintegrates and "all regulation is lacking"; see *Suicide: A Study in Sociology*, translated by John A. Spaulding and George Simpson (Glencoe, Ill., 1951), pp. 252–53. [Editor's note.]

hastened the development of the industrial arts, weapons, communications, and management which facilitated the totalitarian thrust. A considerable elevation in the level of military technology was introduced in the course of the war, and trench warfare on the Western Front was part of an unprecedented deployment of the material means of combat. The reaction of writers like Ernst Jünger to such a "battle of materials" (*Materialschlacht*) became an important element in the postwar disillusionment of intellectuals with traditional values and beliefs. All this adds up to what came to be known as "total mobilization," a kind of absorption of the entire civil population into the war effort, which while not totalitarian (no party; no ideology; no monopoly of communications, weapons, and organizations), yet served as a kind of model, especially in its technical aspects, for the totalitarian orders to come.

Still, the first reaction of the revolutionaries in the central and eastern empires was libertarian, not totalitarian. The battle cries in Russia, Germany, and Austria-Hungary were liberation and freedom, constitutionalism and democracy, and social justice. There has been a very considerable misunderstanding, largely the result of hindsight, of the revolutions of 1917 and 1918.

The Bolshevik Revolution of 1917 was not a totalitarian revolution, nor a revolution intended to establish a totalitarian dictatorship. The regime was conceived in orthodox Marxist terms, as transitional to the new Communist society which was expected to emerge in a relatively short time. But the revolutionaries who seized power with the idea of establishing what Marx had called the "dictatorship of the proletariat" (possibly with the regimes of the two Napoleons in mind) found themselves confronted with a far tougher and more challenging task than they had ever dreamed of. Especially difficult was the problem created by a vast peasantry, entertaining largely preindustrial and precapitalist ideas and providing a formidable stumbling block to that rapid transformation which Marx had envisaged for an advanced industrial society. It is now recognized that the industrialization of the Soviet Union was the key achievement of the revolutionaries. Yet to accomplish this, they had to make maximal use of the political and governmental resources at their disposal; as a result, they fell back upon the inherited traditions and instrumentalities of autocracy. Thus, to illustrate, the tsarist secret police provided a pattern and, in the beginning, even some of the personnel for the party in its struggle to establish an operationally effective regime. But these traditional means proved wholly inadequate, and as a consequence the leaders of the Soviet Union very gradually invented the new techniques that eventually coalesced into what we have called a totalitarian dictatorship.

It is widely believed that this invention is primarily the work of Lenin. To be sure, Lenin, in his famous pamphlet, *What Is To Be Done?* (1902), had expressed the need for an autocratic party—the work has frequently been viewed as a theory of a totalitarian party—harshly disciplined and subject to a single leader. But Lenin's argument was focused upon the requirements imposed by the existing tsarist autocracy: " 'broad democracy' in party organization, amidst the gloom of autocracy . . . is nothing more than a *useless and harmful toy*." [6] Never (to the knowledge of the author) did Lenin prior to the establishment of the Soviet regime say that, having developed such an autocratic party, its permanent adoption by the regime would be desirable. Nor did the Bolsheviks before the revolution ever correspond to what he had written. The early associates of Lenin were rather forceful personalities and Lenin was their inspirational leader. He was not the kind of autocrat who was later to dominate the Soviet Union. There was much vigorous argument and disputa-

[6] V. I. Lenin, *What Is To Be Done?* (New York, 1929), p. 130; the italics are Lenin's. [Editor's note.]

tion. The predominance of Lenin rested upon his extraordinary intellectual power and personality by which he succeeded in integrating the masterful group of revolutionaries associated with him. There was, in short, genuine cooperation; it would have been extraordinary for men fighting the autocracy to have accepted autocracy as a desirable form of government. Totalitarian methods came later and many Communists accepted them only with reluctance. The so-called New Economic Policy (NEP) which Lenin introduced in 1921 was, in fact, a measure of retreat.

The First Five-Year Plan, on the other hand, faced the issue—Stalin's decision to liquidate the peasantry and to destroy the entire class which stood in the way of Communist goals constituted the decisive turn. It had become clear during the first five years of the revolutionary enterprise that the industrialization of the country was the crucial task. This was, moreover, a totally different task from that which Marx had envisaged. Not more equitable distribution, but a vastly increased production became the goal of the masters of the Soviet Union. This question of industrialization preoccupied the regime throughout the twenties and gave the struggle for power among its leadership a marked theoretical flavor. The ensuing policy, however, was based more on the requirements of the situation than on ideology. (The same was to hold true after the Second World War, with minor variations, for the western satellites of the Soviet Union and, even more, for Communist China.) It was the same task that the great mercantilist statesmen of England, France, and elsewhere—the Cecils and the Colberts—had accomplished when they set in motion the industrialization of their countries. Absolute monarchy in their situations sufficed as a pattern of autocracy, partly because the societal transformation, while vast, extended over many generations. The Communists sought to catch up within one generation, and therefore a much more radical deployment of autocratic power was required. This totalitarian breakthrough occurred in 1926–27 when the First Five-Year Plan was adopted. It was this plan that undertook to force the pace and to bring about almost immediately a radical transformation of the economy. Thus, the masters of the Soviet Union were the true originators, the innovators who invented and perfected, in its various details, totalitarian dictatorship—the secret police techniques, the mass communication controls, and more especially, the centrally planned and directed economy.

Fascist—and, later, National Socialist—totalitarianism arose in response to this extraordinary development.

Even though much fraudulent propaganda was involved, there can be little question that a frightened middle class and peasantry were particularly receptive to men and movements that conjured up the specter of an all-engulfing communism: a new kind of society in which all effective political power and control would be in the hands of a proletarian mass party. This frightening prospect was reinforced by the presence in both Italy and Germany of sizable Communist parties of strictly local origin. Though influenced, if not directed, by the Third International at Moscow, they were deeply rooted in the Marxist tradition of a proletarian movement that was nearly a century old. These Communist parties pointed to the example of the Soviet Union with increasing pride, calling it "the workers' paradise." They went readily along with the Soviet regime in justifying and, indeed, glorifying the turn toward totalitarianism.

When in 1922 Mussolini seized power in Italy, he had no conception of a totalitarian dictatorship, even though the word "total" soon became a favorite with him. His became a dictatorship typically devoted to "conserving" and protecting Italy from the Communists. But there were more radical revolutionary forces at work in the

Duce's following, and eventually he turned to totalitarian methods, though never carrying them very far until encouraged by the Nazi seizure of power.

The Nazis, too, expressed no desire to erect a totalitarian regime, though Hitler in his melodramatic extremism tended toward totalitarian rhetoric. His regime, nevertheless, became totalitarian much faster than Mussolini's and Stalin's, partly because he could proceed on the basis of fifteen years' experience. Hitler came to power in January, 1933. The effective breakthrough may possibly be placed in 1936 when comprehensive economic planning was first adopted, though markedly totalitarian methods had been adopted as early as 1934 in the bloody suppression of the leftist opposition in the Roehm Putsch. Now, it might be argued that Hitler's movement was in a sense an outgrowth of the war. Certainly, the Versailles Treaty provided him with a major point of attack in discrediting the democratic regime of the Weimar Republic. (And one might add, for good measure, that Hitler's rabidly autocratic propensities had been nourished by his war experience as described in *Mein Kampf*.) It has been said that Hitler's violent demagogy could not have fallen on such fertile ground if the values and beliefs of German society had not been so profoundly weakened by the catastrophe of the lost war and the virtual destruction of the middle class by the war-begotten inflation.

We have already alluded to the *anomie*, the disintegration of the convictional core which produced an intellectual vacuum, an emotional homelessness. Into this vacuum moved the totalitarian movements of both right and left, of Fascists, Nazis, and Communists, with their appeals to violent overthrow of the established order. There can be little question that total ideologies thrived in such soil and gained fanatical adherents, including many uprooted intellectuals. Novels and other writings of the period amply demonstrate the point. Hence, even though the war and its consequences may not entirely explain the rise of totalitarianism, they certainly contributed their share. The contrast of the situation after the Second World War, with its Marshall Plan, economic miracles, and affluent societies, highlights the point.

III

But there is a spiritual context to this problem of totalitarianism that deserves special attention. It provides further support for the thesis that the First World War and totalitarianism are joint products of related forces in Western society rather than cause and effect.

In the second half of the nineteenth century, a new intellectual pessimism began to spread through Europe. Voices like Arthur Schopenhauer's were followed by Jacob Burckhardt's and Friedrich Nietzsche's. It was a pessimism rooted in the conviction that the very foundations of culture and spirit were being undermined by modern technology and mass civilization. Poets and writers like Feodor Dostoevsky and Maurice Barrès contributed to this mood. That man was becoming uprooted and alienated, robbed of his very soul, could no longer be overcome or transcended in these circles by an optimistic faith in a social revolution and its Elysian aftermath.

In a way, the most influential, and at the same time the most mordant, of these troubled spirits was Nietzsche. He had visions that foreshadowed the world of totalitarianism in spite of the absence of any specific prediction of totalitarian dictatorship. It was a vision of a state of mind rather than an institutional and governmental setup. And it is not to be found in Nietzsche's familiar doctrine of the "superman," who in Nietzsche's own vision was not a totalitarian dictator, but rather a philosopher. There occurs, however, a passage in his most celebrated, his most poetic and visionary work, *Thus Spake Zarathustra* (1883–

85), about another kind of man—the "last man." It is this man that is relevant to Nietzsche's prophetic vision of a totalitarian universe. In this work we find an atmosphere of all-engulfing pessimism characteristic of the seedbed of fascist totalitarianism. This is what Nietzsche wrote:

> Behold I show you the last man. What is love? What is creation? What is a star? Thus the last man asketh blinking. Then earth will have become small and on it the last man will be hopping who maketh everything small. His species is indestructible like that of the sand flea; the last man liveth longest.[7]

In sentiments such as these a bitter and poisonous cynicism was distilled and spread. Is it without significance that this work of Nietzsche's was carried in the knapsacks of the German volunteers who died in the fields of Flanders? There is, of course, much truth in what Nietzsche wrote; we all recognize the mass society of the twentieth century in such a passage. In its nether regions it does indeed resemble what Nietzsche rebelled against. But there is no recognition of the constructive potential of the welfare state and the affluent society, of the intrinsic human values implied in a war against poverty, exploitation, and discrimination.

What is embodied in Nietzsche's vision of the last man is a kind of esthetic revulsion at efforts by, and on behalf of, the common man. This bitter negative utopia, this "disutopia," as one might call it, flowered after the war in the nightmare worlds described in the novels of Aldous Huxley and George Orwell. American writers such as H. L. Mencken echoed these sentiments—Mencken had been deeply influenced by Nietzsche. The intellectual atmosphere created by these views was not favorable to the maintenance, let alone the growth, of solid convictions regarding the freedom and the dignity of the common

[7] Friedrich Nietzsche, *Thus Spake Zarathustra,* translated by Alexander Tille (New York, 1902), pp. 11–12. [Editor's note.]

man. Indeed, one is tempted to speak of a crisis of democracy. Thorstein Veblen may be cited in this connection: "The common man is constantly and increasingly exposed to the risks of becoming an undesirable citizen in the eyes of the votaries of law and order." In a very real sense Nietzsche, an esthete critical of democratic society, placed himself on the side of the "votaries of law and order." It is clear that the First World War furthered, by its vast destruction of traditional institutions and values, the very spiritual chaos which had helped to bring it on. No wonder that some of the reactive and sensitive spirits returned from the war with ardent revolutionary visions of a total reconstruction of society.

To conclude on a note which is more specifically political and which in a way epitomizes the argument presented here: what cannot be emphasized too much is the tragic incapacity of the victors of the war to achieve real peace. Having set out to win a "war to end all wars," they ended up by fashioning treaties that were incapable of surviving for very long. This incapacity to achieve peace, which in retrospect seems quite extraordinary, was a direct result of the total mobilization engendered by the war. If one studies English public opinion in 1917–18, one finds it quite moderate and sensible, ready for a real peace. By 1919, demagogues had gotten the upper hand and such a peace was no longer possible. It is a sad story, and this is not the place to tell it. But the inability to reach that state of peace (which Spinoza once so beautifully characterized as not merely the absence of war, but the presence of a positive spirit and a fortitude of mind) resulted from the fact that the total mobilization and propaganda of the war had created violently destructive emotions and completely misleading stereotypes of the opposing nations and of the human beings who comprised them. Since the victors viewed the vanquished as subhuman, they could engage in the sadistic orgies implied in such slogans as "squeeze the orange until the pips squeak." The postwar fiasco suggests that the war in this respect also set the stage for the rise of totalitarianism. We have already spoken of the use Hitler made of the Versailles Treaty. There were many more subtle lines of influence which led from the "non-peace" to totalitarian dictatorship: the failure to create something viable in place of the Habsburg Empire, the stimulation given to Italian chauvinism, the rejection of the League of Nations by the United States.

In short, the First World War appears to be a link in the chain of "causes" which constitute the history of the rise of totalitarian dictatorship. It is part and parcel of the story, no more, no less. It was not the primary moving force. That force was provided by revolutionary movements reaching back beyond the war into the nineteenth century. These movements have since become worldwide. Yet for Europe and the world at large, World War I ended an epoch. It is today acknowledged by all that the centuries of European predominance then came to an end. They will never return. The United States and the Soviet Union have become the bearers of two divergent strands of European political culture: constitutionalism and autocracy, both claiming the mantle of democracy. Which will eventually prevail, no scientific analysis is at present able to predict. But it seems probable, in the light of the spread of autocracy after the Second World War, that a third holocaust would give totalitarian autocracy the upper hand and would universalize totalitarianism.

In such a perspective, the experience of the First World War is indeed instructive. But will not war itself once again be the consequence as much as the cause of the spread of totalitarianism?

5 THE TRANSFORMATION OF AMERICAN LIFE

Charles Hirschfeld

For Americans who lived through it, World War I is a memory swathed in emotion. Some fondly remember the spell that Woodrow Wilson cast on them as he exhorted the best minds of the country to take counsel with him and follow him to the uplands of clear light where moral certitude shone. When war came, these idealists of old-line American stock eagerly responded to Wilson's appeal and answered the call to overseas adventure or joined the crusade to remake the world in the image of America. For other Americans of foreign birth, the war was a never-forgotten nightmare in which the news came to the slums that a son who had been drafted had been killed in action in France and a father's grief turned to hatred of the war, Wilson, and the world.

When American historians of the next generation came to write what have become the standard general accounts of the war, they too responded with strong emotion. Despite their claims to toughminded realism, through a haze of disillusion and pacifism they saw the war as a tragic error: Americans, high and low, had been gulled by Allied duplicity and lured into the conflict by mercenary capitalists, their own greed, as well as by their misguided, self-appointed role as moral policemen of the world. These historians ruefully chronicled the crusade, almost millennial in its hopes to crush autocracy and make the world safe for democracy, as the very climax of the progressive battle against the evil bosses in the Wilhelmstrasse. They dwelt with irony on the patriotic exaltation with which the American people carried on the war, on the adolescent flexing of muscles in belligerent brag ("the Yanks are coming and it will soon be over, over there"). With the bittersweet relish of the enlightened, they detailed the fury against the Hun and Kaiser Bill and the hysteria which engulfed dissenters, as the strangers in the land became the enemy within the gates.

More or less explicitly, these accounts passed judgment on the war as essentially something Americans ought to be ashamed of, a quixotic foray into world affairs and a disgraceful emotional debauch which led inevitably to bitter disillusion and which sidetracked and eventually destroyed the truly American and altogether realistic ideals of the Progressive movement. This judgment was complemented by the canonization of those men who stood steadfast against the war: Senator La Follette, who like an angry prophet cried out that it would destroy reform at home; Senator Norris, who refused to put the dollar sign on the American flag; and Randolph Bourne, who turned his humped back on the intellectuals who rationalized their support of the war. In this view, the war was at bottom a betrayal of the American dream, an overblown expression of the American mission which brought only the conquest of high ideals by sordid realities and the cynical philistinism of the twenties, from which the people were fortunately rescued by the evangelical fervor of the New Deal and the war against the fascist hordes.

The above is perhaps a greatly simplified summary of

what might be called the standard liberal historiography of the American war experience. Certainly, in recent years, histories of the war have moved in the direction of greater realism and broader perspective. Some of the basic animadversion, nonetheless, still runs through many of them, and American participation in the war still seems, by some transcendental standard, to require extenuation; it is represented as the best that could be done in a very difficult situation and besides, it was not exactly an American choice, the decision for war having rested with the Germans. From the vantage of the brave new world of the sixties, even the revised version seems in its own way parochial and smacks of apologetics.

To balance the account, it is necessary to take a larger view of America's role in the war, along the lines of Professor Allan Nevins' hope that America's projection into world leadership would be "in some fashion connected . . . with the advent of the age of mass action, mass production, and mass psychology in American life." [1] It is first necessary to take a synoptic view of American history of the last seventy-five years. The detailed periodization into the Agrarian Crusade, the imperialist interlude, the Progressive Era, Boom and Bust, the New Deal, World War II, the Fair Deal, and the Cold War, while useful for some purposes, blurs some basic long-term trends. Taking the period as a whole, one may see that World War I was the first important and intensive phase in a fairly continuous development, indeed as a harbinger of the present, an auspice of what the country has become today. One might say that it was for the United States the beginning of the twentieth century, the era of American leadership in a world of wars and international crises, of the global economy, the leviathan state, the mass society, and the age of anxiety.

[1] Allan Nevins, "Should American History Be Rewritten?" *Saturday Review of Literature*, XXXVII (February 6, 1954), 47.

I

Today, the United States is a world power pursuing its national interest and ideals on a global scale by means of diplomacy, force, economics, and ideological weapons. As the greatest power in the world, it cannot be officially indifferent to the international balance of forces. As W. W. Rostow has said,

> There is nothing in the national interest or in the American creed which demands that we dominate the rest of the world; but there is much in our tradition and our way of life which requires that we be the defender and promoter of the democratic cause on the world scene. . . . The American interest is to preserve an environment for our free, open, and humanistic society which will permit it to continue to develop in terms of [its] fundamental values [political, social, and economic]. . . .[2]

World War I was the first crucial expression of this policy. In a period of four or five years, between 1914 and 1918, the United States first assumed this posture *vis à vis* the world in a conscious, if not always clear and unfaltering way.

This was more so the case than at the turn of the century, during the years of the Spanish-American War and colonial imperialism. There was a forced and unreal quality to that experience, as though America were acting out a part in a script that had been written for others. There was an element of romantic rebellion in that early expansionist surge that transcended the imperatives of reality. It was but a brief interlude in which no overwhelming threats forced immediate and decisive responses. And the same observation may be made about most of Theodore Roosevelt's excursions, verbal and actual, into the international arena.

[2] W. W. Rostow, "International Prospects under the New President," *Massachusetts Review*, II (1961), 202, 203.

But during the First World War, the United States emerged, beyond dispute, as a world power with interests and obligations of its own to defend and fulfill. As a major economic and naval power by 1914, it was forced into the continuous testing of its assumptions and choices against unpleasant realities. Realistically and objectively speaking, that is, looking at the results of actions as well as at the expressed motives thereof, one may say that the United States intervened in the European war in its own national interest. That interest lay in a balance of power in the world that would be conducive to a peaceful and generally stable international polity, the necessary condition for continued American development. This policy of realism was, of course, fused with the idealistic motive of fostering and preserving democracy in Europe: Only in a world where the powers great and small enjoyed liberal democratic institutions could there obtain the peaceful international relations in which America could prosper in its own way of life.

The United States moved to achieve its goal along two lines of approach: by positive intervention to stop the war and thus stay out of it, or, failing that, by going to war. The first approach was embodied in American efforts at mediation, to bring about a negotiated peace between the belligerents on the basis of a reasonable, balanced settlement, a peace without victory, or, if you will, a stalemate. As Colonel House made clear, the primary purpose of such mediation was to keep either side from so crushing the other as to destroy a viable balance of power—a balance viable, that is, in terms of American interests and security. Specifically, mediation was necessary not only to keep Germany from crushing Great Britain, but also to prevent an overwhelming Allied victory that would leave an aggressively imperialist Russia dominant in Europe. This approach, it is important to note, engaged the pacific idealism of many Americans, including President Wilson's, who combined his pursuit of peace with an ideological crusade to uphold the sanctity of international law as well as the abstract tradition of neutrality.

The second approach was directed toward preventing a German victory by openly associating American interest with that of the Allies. This policy was undergirded by a strong democratic idealism which equated Germany with autocracy, and therefore, with the ideological adversary. It appealed to the more aggressive nationalists like Theodore Roosevelt and Secretary Lansing who wished to adopt it from the early days of the war. Wilson, however, demurred as long as he could until his hand was forced.

What forced his hand was the context in which American foreign policy had been developing over a period of twenty-five years before the war—the Anglo-American rapprochement, in which from 1895 on, the two countries had found themselves coming together in the face of the threat of growing German aggressive intentions. The American community of interests with Great Britain—a community of political, economic, strategic, as well as cultural interests of the two great dominant powers—rested on the maintenance of the international status quo and on the mutual acceptance of British naval supremacy in the Atlantic and American hegemony in the Caribbean. It was this tacit understanding, verging on commitment, that made any real neutrality impossible and brought the United States to the aid of the Allies in an economic way from the beginning of the war. It led America to accept, despite serious irritations, the claims of British sea power. The United States went along with the effective blockade of Germany and refrained from breaking it, considering such action to be unneutral and against all dictates of American policy, with no gain for the national interest. For two years, Wilson warded off in the name of international law any effective German submarine attacks on his country's trade with the Allies, thus ensuring the flow of munitions and food. American support of the Allies was thus not some contingency which snowballed haphazardly into irresistible compulsion. It was attuned to the long-range national interest which from the beginning changed the instinct for neutrality into a benevolent neutrality that was not really neutrality at all but an active, if non-belligerent, participation leading in the end to full military involvement.

When the belligerents persisted in pressing for a knockout blow—the Allies refusing to negotiate for peace and the Germans resorting to unrestricted submarine warfare—they rendered nugatory the policy of mediation. The greater threat of a German victory now compelled the United States to act in its own interest to prevent it. In the decision for war, Wilson thus shifted to the second approach, the very position of his bitter opponent, Roosevelt. At the same time, he wriggled out of the ambiguities and unreality of his defense of outmoded international law and put American belligerency on the highest idealistic plane by picturing it as a struggle to bring about a stable and peaceful international order. He appealed to Americans to go to war for the purpose of creating the conditions of permanent peace, an international community that would destroy once and for all the balance of power system. This is what he meant when he declared that America would fight to make the world safe for democracy. Characteristically, the idea of a League of Nations became for him the ultimate counter-demonstration to the ugly realities of war and power politics.

And yet the idea of a league was also rooted in the realities of national interest. It was originally held out as an inducement to coax Great Britain to agree to a negotiated peace. It was considered as an instrument for controlling national power in the best interests of the United States, using the nucleus of Anglo-American strength to create a cooperative international order. When the United States declared war, the League was firmly tied to military victory over a Prussian autocracy which was the chief obstacle to the desired end.

All during the war, moreover, American diplomacy continued to be shaped by consciousness of a distinctive national interest. America did not adopt the Allied war aims. It considered itself only an "associated power." It did not wish to see Germany beaten into helplessness. Its ultimate aim was a league which would include Germany and at the same time end the British control of the seas that had so strongly irritated the country in 1916, and which would create a concert of all the powers cooperating to maintain the peace.

American foreign policy in the First World War was thus a fairly effective fusion of ideals and self-interest. The course of its unfolding was not, however, as clear and straightforward as here outlined. There was confusion of purpose and conflict over means. There were new and incredibly complicated and dangerous situations to deal with. American public opinion, untutored, idealistic, isolationist, pro-Ally but opposed to war, had to be brought along step by step. Wilson himself shared many of the hopes, fears, and uncertainties of his people. He was indeed torn between rival ends and means. While not unaware of the material interests involved—which his closest advisers, House and Lansing, insistently called to his attention—he was loath to recognize the part they played in the determination of policy. He was fundamentally an idealist who hated war and sincerely believed in the American mission to fight for the right and to bring democracy and peace to a war-torn world. He was the leader who together with his people faced the dilemma of all men of good will in all times—that of trying to reconcile the brute world of fact with the ideals of men, of recognizing the demands of reality while still trying to keep them within moral bounds.

In the First World War, in summation, the United States had its necessary interests. It had its cherished ideals. And it had the raw power. But it was not always sure how to use its power to realize its interests and preserve and promote its ideals. It learned slowly and painfully and took a giant step into the twentieth century.

II

American power was then, as now, largely rooted in its economic strength. Today, the United States is indisputably the greatest economic power in the world and its economy is integrated with that of the rest of the world. This global primacy was first attained and exploited during, and as a result of, World War I. Under pressure of that crisis, the United States surpassed all the great European powers in industrial production, financial strength, and foreign trade. It was the economic mainstay of the struggle against Germany. As American exports poured out across the Atlantic and European investments in the New World were liquidated, the United States passed from being a debtor nation to a creditor nation and became the greatest source of capital in the world. New York replaced London as the world's financial center. The loans extended to the Allies on the government as well as on private account amounted to more than twelve billion dollars. American foreign trade expanded enormously, not only with the Allies, but also at their expense. The United States was well on its way to becoming the chief supplier of agricultural commodities and manufactured goods for world markets as well as the greatest consumer of raw materials in the world.

Domestically, the gross national product almost doubled during the war years, and the country as a whole reached new heights of prosperity. The boom developed in the context of tremendously increased government expenditures, which were about twenty-five times greater by 1919 than they had been in 1914. Most of this outlay was, of course, for military purposes, and constituted about 25 per cent of the national income. It was these enormous governmental expenditures that were probably responsible for the great changes in the quantity and quality of the American economic and social order. The experience was similar to that of the last twenty years, in which, as sociologist Daniel Bell has argued, it was not so much the New Deal measures of the thirties as the gigantic government capital outlays since 1945, especially for national security, that have revolutionized American society, released the country's productive energies, and made for the purposeful management of the economy.

The large-scale fiscal intervention during World War I was accompanied by government regulatory and planning measures to a degree previously unparalleled in American history. Such measures effected an almost total mobilization of the economy and earned the epithet of "war socialism" from its opponents. The federal government became the director and even at times the dictator of the economy for the sake of increased industrial output. The War Industries Board mobilized the industrial machine, controlled prices, and enforced priorities in the supply of raw materials and in the distribution of the finished products. Foreign trade and domestic capital investments were controlled and subsidized; consumption of fuel and food was regulated and rationed. The Railroad Administration took over and ran the nation's railroads as a unified transportation system. The War Labor Board guaranteed, for the first time in the history of American national policy, the labor unions' right to collective bargaining and enforced the eight-hour day and the principle of the "living wage." When one company insisted on requiring its workers to sign yellow-dog contracts, the War Department commandeered its plant. High federal taxes were levied in an attempt, not wholly successful, to prevent excessive profiteering. Along with the consolidation and centralization of powers in the federal government, the war advanced the process of industrial concentration—to the point of oligopoly in some cases—and thus was an important step toward the domination of the economy by giant corporate units.

There was, in short, during the war years a substantial amalgamation of the private and public sectors of the economy for the sake of the more efficient prosecution of the war. At the same time, there were significant beginnings of what C. Wright Mills has called "administrative liberalism," in which the welfare of the people, particularly the underprivileged, was protected and advanced by continuous, administrative process of executive agencies of the government. Such developments, and the possibilities of carrying them further into peacetime, brought a number of reformers and progressives around to the support of the Wilson Administration and the war. They felt that the domestic war measures as well as Wilson's foreign policies were important steps in the direction of a progressive, nationalized social order as they conceived it. The historian William E. Leuchtenburg has even maintained that the wartime experience was as great an influence on the New Deal as the Progressive movement.[3] He has shown that much of the legislation of the thirties was directly based on the earlier war measures, and that many of the men who supported and administered such New Deal measures as the NRA and the NLRB had been officials in the corresponding wartime agencies, not the least of whom was Franklin D. Roosevelt himself. Beyond that, it is tolerably clear that what Max Lerner has called "the amalgamation of state capitalism and business

[3] William E. Leuchtenburg, "The New Deal and the Analogue of War," in John Braeman *et al.*, *Change and Continuity in Twentieth-Century America* (Columbus, Ohio, 1965), pp. 81–143.

collectivism" is a development to the greatest degree of the inchoate efforts of 1915–19.

It might here be suggested that the two great developments so far touched on—the emergence of the United States as a world power and the evolution of the positive interventionist state, two great themes which were as basic to the Wilson Administration as they are to American society today—could not and, in fact, did not evolve in compartmented isolation from one another; there has been, indeed, a positive and reciprocal relationship between them for the last seventy-five years. To a greater degree than is usually suspected, America's involvement in world affairs has been responsible for the radical changes in its social, political, and economic system. The experience of World War I was the first clear embodiment of this organic relationship which, though obscured in the twenties and thirties, emerged strongly once again when the country was faced, in World War II, with the threat to its survival. The last twenty years of the Cold War have deepened and intensified the relationship to the point where the distinctions between foreign and domestic policy have tended to break down altogether.

III

A new American nation came into being during the war. The intense experience greatly furthered the nationalization of American life and gave the American people a real sense of unity. Many of the processes that have created the consolidated, homogeneous (some would say, regimented and conformist), and national-continental society of the sixties are to be found operating in some degree in the years between 1917 and 1919.

For almost a century before 1914, American society had been kept in a state of flux by the rapid, wasteful exploitation of the country's natural resources, by the westward movement, and by the waves of immigrants that inundated its shores. Not until the twentieth century had there been a perceptible mitigation of the intensity of these disruptive forces. And World War I was a decisive step in the restoration of stability, national unity, and even a measure of *gemeinschaft*.

It is often forgotten that until 1900, the United States was not a completed continental unit in the physical sense. There were great empty spaces in the land that were not even settled or that were only emerging from primitive isolation. The country was a loosely tied parcel of diverse sections in varying stages of development. In studying their history, Americans tend to project into the past the current conception of the settled, integrated continental community. It was something of a shock, for example, to read, in Professor Mark Schorer's exhaustive and exhausting biography,[4] that Sinclair Lewis' native village of Sauk Center, Minnesota, had been, only two decades before his birth in 1885, barren prairie. Whole sections of the Great Plains, the Rocky Mountain states, the Southwest, and the Pacific Northwest were as yet unpeopled or undeveloped and could hardly have been said to exist as substantive elements of the national life. Not until the second decade of the twentieth century did these waste spaces begin to fill up and develop, and not until recently was the process completed by the emergence of megalopolitan areas.

The first two decades of the new century, and not the nineties, saw the end of the westward movement and the significant backwash to the cities and then to the suburbs of America. The result was a new and different kind of mobility. Americans still remained the most mobile people in the world. But they were no longer going out on errands into the wilderness or "lighting out for the Territory";

[4] Mark Schorer, *Sinclair Lewis: An American Life* (New York, 1961), p. 4.

they were moving into better-paying jobs and the mushrooming suburbs. This was still mobility, but oh! the difference.

As the country was rounded out and was knit into a national economic unity, the force of sectionalism was greatly weakened. Sectionalism in the nineteenth century, with its etymological suggestion of cutting, was a radical, divisive force that produced the bloody trauma of the Civil War and the fury of the agrarian crusade. In the war years, its force was greatly attenuated. What replaced it was what is now called regionalism, a word with much milder connotations. As such, differing geographical, as well as pluralistic, group interests took their place within the national, political-economic framework. They were accommodated within the inclusive continental nationalism or found outlets in the expansive supranationalism of the war effort. The resentments of the wheat growers against wartime ceilings on the price of their product or the generally isolationist sentiment of the Middle West never erupted into radical, disjunctive political movements.

The First World War halted the flood of European immigration to this country and was followed by its virtual prohibition by law in the twenties. Thus, for the first time in American history, the great variety of ethnic and national strains were able to coalesce. The melting pot had a chance to work without constant infusions of new ingredients, and American society had a chance to jell. The war hastened the process of Americanization, sometimes by coercion, and the wartime prosperity gave the immigrants and their children the opportunity to rise in the social scale and assimilate to the older norms of American society —not, to be sure, without transforming them. And not without protest from the native-born at what must have seemed to them the spread of alien ways.

The war also stimulated the first large-scale migration of the Negroes out of the South. Half a million made their way to northeastern and midwestern industrial centers and another half million were uprooted from their homes by the draft. Disruptive though this movement may have been, it was the substantial beginning of improvement in the Negroes' economic status and of their absorption, not without violent—and still continuing—strains, into the American community at large.

The war effort also brought, for the first time, large numbers of intellectuals into the government machinery and into institutional roles generally. The men who, in C. Wright Mills' definition, deal in symbols of communication, create states of consciousness, and live *for* and not *off* ideas, were recruited into government service in great numbers. Historians, economists, political scientists, and psychologists, as well as writers, journalists, actors, and artists, found themselves serving the great leviathan and forwarding the national purpose—a phenomenon that was to grow and reach its culmination in the last twenty years. There were some intellectuals, of course, who were alienated by the war and found it a damper on creative activity—independent writers and artists like Randolph Bourne, Alfred Kreymborg, John Sloan, and Alfred Stieglitz—but their numbers were small.

What the intellectuals in the service of the nation at war reflected and fostered was a distinct sense of national unity, which bound up the loosened social ties of the previous decade and drew off its discontents. They articulated the national purpose for millions, giving voice to the idealism of the historical American mission. They purveyed the printed and spoken word to put men and minds in uniform. Some of the progressives among them wholeheartedly supported the war effort, if only because they felt that it united the nation in one increasing purpose, which for them was the great desideratum worth achieving at all costs.

And there was a cost—in illiberalism, intolerance, and

the suppression of freedom of speech and opinion—as Wilson himself had foreseen. The nationalization of American life did not take place without great injury to American democratic ideals. But the hysteria which prevailed was precisely an indication of the extent and intensity of the wartime departure from the traditional American norms. It was a measure of the travail of the American community in the face of the new exigencies. It was not only the aliens, pacifists, and radical dissenters who suffered calumny, suppression, and torture. Their suppressors and calumniators also suffered as they witnessed the subversion of the old America and its transformation under pressure into a new order of things. They took out their frustration at having to stand by and watch the inevitable erosion of their ideals and way of life on the helpless scapegoats who so conveniently offered themselves to hand. This social-psychological phenomenon was to be repeated more recently in our own and other lands, and with greater intensity and cruelty.

America, in short, was being welded into a new nation by the pressure of international crisis and war; and many Americans were not ready to accept the new order, but sought to stay with irrational vindictiveness what could not in fact be stayed.

IV

The whole traditional American way of life seemed to be under concerted attack. To many Americans, it appeared that the nation was caught up in the toils of international intrigue and "our boys" were, as a result, dying on foreign shores. The economy prospered in unholy fashion: profits skyrocketed; labor strutted in striped silk shirts; women flocked to the factories and offices; and farmers reveled in two-dollar wheat. The self-contained, rural and small-town white, Anglo-Saxon, Protestant America of a century past seemed to be sinking beneath the flood of the new and the strange. But it was not only the visible world that shook and was foundering. The war was above all an assault on the moral order of nineteenth-century America, on the very cement of society and, indeed, of the universe. The hysteria directed against the "Huns" and the aliens and the pacifists was not merely an overflow of bellicosity, but a reaction to the whole process of change that was destroying the old order, its ideals and values.

The hold of the past was still strong. Nostalgia for a world beyond recall and even beyond reality ruled the hearts of many old-line Americans. Once the war was over, this nostalgia came to the surface in a most vicious way. The return to normalcy was more than a retreat into isolation, more than a reaction to an exaggerated idealism. It was a scurrying back to the shelter of traditional American verities. The Red Scare, Prohibition, the Ku Klux Klan were at once attacks on the forces of evil that were rotting the American way and attempts by legal and extralegal means to restore it.

The moral predicament of the American people, their malaise over the shattering of belief, was clearly expressed in the postwar novels. Hemingway and Fitzgerald crystallized in an unforgettable way the mood of America at war. For, it must be noted, these writers were not merely footloose expatriates sunk in *anomie* on the Left Bank or sybarites cavorting to the jazz of Babylon on Long Island Sound. They were, indeed, Americans from the heartland, from Oak Park and St. Paul. For them, the war had destroyed all traditional values. It had led to the betrayal of the old ideals by the basest inhuman acts. They were thus left in a world without values. This was the point of departure in their novels, what they took for granted. To reconstitute the old morality or elaborate a new one was clearly out of the question. All they could do was to evoke a moral style, a mood and a posture of some dignity and decency. As Jake Barnes said, "I did not care what it was all about. All I wanted to know was how to live in it." "What is moral is what you feel good after," and not dirty or false, Hemingway himself concluded.[5] That such diffuse yearning might eventually degenerate into the mud-bed of moral clichés was an ominious, if then unsuspected, possibility.

The search for a moral style was directed by nostalgia. Always, a dream of the good life haunted Hemingway: the idyll of the Big Two-Hearted River in the peaceful forests of Michigan's Upper Peninsula of his youth or the vision of the shaded walks of Oak Park. He knew it could not be brought back, but evoking it made him feel good, if very sad.

Fitzgerald was likewise haunted. Nick Caraway, listening to Gatsby, hears with the mind's ear "an elusive rhythm," "a fragment of lost words that I had heard somewhere a long time ago." [6] Fitzgerald, with more penetration than Hemingway, felt and expressed the great paradox that faced the wartime generation. He liked to believe that the American Dream could be realized through money and power and ambition. But he also sensed that these were the very source of the corruption of the beauty and integrity of that Dream. And he faced up to what he saw as the truth of our national life—"so much raw power . . . haunted by envisioned romance," as Lionel Trilling has put it.

Here, in a few words, is the essence of the dilemma faced by the American people in the war: a colossal power bestriding the world, yet loath to accept this reality and haunted always by the simple, noble ideal of its past—how to reconcile the raw reality with the noble dream, the

[5] Ernest Hemingway, *The Sun Also Rises* (New York, 1954), p. 118; *Death in the Afternoon* (New York, 1932), p. 4.

[6] F. Scott Fitzgerald, *The Great Gatsby* (New York, 1953), p. 112.

power with the glory. Fitzgerald has movingly evoked the tragic predicament:

> And as the moon rose higher the inessential houses began to melt away until gradually I became aware of the old island here that flowered once for Dutch sailors' eyes—a fresh, green breast of the new world. Its vanished trees, the trees that had made way for Gatsby's house, had once pandered in whispers to the last and greatest of human dreams; for a transitory enchanted moment man must have held his breath in the presence of this continent, compelled into an aesthetic contemplation he neither understood nor desired, face to face for the last time in history with something commensurate to his capacity for wonder.
>
> And as I sat there brooding on the old, unknown world, I thought of Gatsby's wonder when he first picked out the green light at the end of Daisy's dock. He had come a long way to this blue lawn, and his dream must have seemed so close that he could hardly fail to grasp it. He did not know that it was already behind him, somewhere back in that vast obscurity beyond the city, where the dark fields of the republic rolled on under the night.
>
> Gatsby believed in the green light, the orgiastic future that year by year recedes before us. It eluded us then, but that's no matter—tomorrow we will run faster, stretch out our arms farther. . . . And one fine morning———
>
> So we beat on, boats against the current, borne back ceaselessly into the past.[7]

[7] *Ibid.*, p. 182.

6 CONCLUSION: THE FIRST WORLD WAR AS A TURNING POINT

Jack J. Roth

What clearly emerges from the foregoing essays is that the meaning of the First World War cannot be restricted either in time or in place, for what is most significant about the war did not "begin" in 1914 or "end" in 1918. Nor was the war's impact confined to the battlefield or even to Europe. Moreover, the war appears to have been no mere "catalyst" accelerating prewar tendencies. The notion of war as a simple catalyst implies a wholly unwarranted determinism. The war not only facilitated change, it played a powerful role in molding its quality and strength. This view of the war suggests its pivotal role in directing the destinies of the contemporary world—it is in this sense that the war was possibly a "turning point."

The role of the First World War as turning point is a problem in historical synthesis. As such, it requires broad focus and sharp delineation. It is the purpose of this essay to attempt both—first, from the standpoint of international politics, and second, from the point of view of European values and institutions.

I

In international politics, within Europe and between Europe and the world, the war worked a profound transformation. In virtually all instances, however, the roots of change are found in the prewar years. But their existence was largely unsuspected or ignored. Even more extraordinary, notwithstanding the shock of the war, was the fact that the transformation during the postwar era was so unclear to contemporaries.

* * *

The war introduced and passed on the phenomenon of "total war" as legacy to the interwar period. Absolute totality—a war of annihilation—was then, of course, technically impossible. What was unique about the war and what it appeared to "fix" was the idea and practice of unrestricted warfare, of escalation of both means and ends without apparent limit.

The historic preparation for unrestricted warfare took place well in advance of 1914. In the wars of the French Revolution, in their popular basis and ideological goals, there already was much that pointed in this direction. But the war-making potential of the eighteenth-century state was still comparatively limited. Decisive developments came with the nineteenth century: the extraordinary growth in population made possible the mobilization of armies on an unprecedented scale, and the expansion of industry and innovations in military technology enormously extended the potential for destruction. Thus, the manipulation and management of both men and resources in an age of mass politics could now make warfare a far more profound social experience. In the American Civil War and even in the Boer War—both stalemated conflicts—the perceptive observer could find hints of the future. If the wars of the nineteenth century were limited it was because they remained localized, quickly resolved, and never became ideological. The Prussian wars of 1866 and 1870 were universally assumed to be models for future conflict. And herein lay the significance of the Franco-Russian alliance of 1894 and the Schlieffen Plan of a decade later. They raised the danger of a general war. But a general war without rapid victory threatened to bring into play revolutionary forces maturing for more than a century.

What made World War I incalculable and uncontrollable was the unexpected deadlock that followed the Battle of the Marne in September, 1914. An approximate balance of military power and the superiority of the defensive was largely responsible for the military stalemate. And the failure of the military was followed by a failure in statesmanship, with neither side willing to make important concessions. Germany had the immediate advantages, but in a long war the Entente was favored. When the war became irreversible, escalation seemed the only way out of the impasse.

The mounting fury of the war, however, was no mere question of the number of casualties or even of the extension of warfare to civilians, but of a readiness to risk the entire order of European life—anything—to win the war. It was the Russian determination to persevere, regardless of frightful losses, that resulted in the collapse of March, 1917. It was the decision of the German High Command to resort to unrestricted submarine warfare (Walter Rathenau called it "a leap into an abyss") that brought the United States into the war. It was the insistence of the Allies and the determination of the Russian Provisional Government to continue the war that made the position of the new regime untenable. It was the decision of the German High Command to arrange Lenin's return to Russia that created an essential condition for the success of the Bolshevik coup. It was the Allied intervention, beginning as an attempt to reopen the Eastern Front, that all but guaranteed the survival of the Bolshevik regime.

The war, in fact, ended everywhere in incitement to revolution. Wilson and the Allies made revolution—the breakup of the Austrian and Ottoman empires and the overthrow of the Hohenzollern—a condition of peace. Lenin demanded the war be transformed into a revolutionary uprising aimed at the total destruction of the prewar European order. Viewed in this light, the determination to use all available weapons, to fight to the bitter end or to win a complete military victory had immeasurable consequences. The American intervention, the revolution in Russia, the "Balkanization" of Europe, and the possibility of a revolutionary tidal wave that might engulf victor and vanquished alike were the fruits of total war. Needless to say, these cataclysmic consequences had hardly been foreseen or desired by the statesmen who went to war in 1914.

The war created the conviction that total war, war without limitation, had possibly been fixed as the pattern for future international conflict. To be sure, some military leaders might look to mechanization to restore the offensive, others to the deterrent of elaborate defensive fortifications. But the postwar era, among civilian and military leaders alike, was to be dominated by the presumed "lessons" of the war. And foremost among these was the conviction that in the future no political system was likely to survive defeat, and that the "next war" might even mean annihilation. In Germany, Ludendorff and the Nazis widely propagated the notion that the new era of total war required a drastic reordering of the community and the construction of an "armed state." Soviet military doctrine, without extolling the virtues of war, amounted to the same thing.

During the twenties the fear of the imminent recurrence of total war receded, only to mount rapidly in the thirties.

The Nazi and Soviet regimes were by the mid-thirties organized to meet such a danger. The Nazis particularly threatened to unleash it. What Hitler sought, however, were the fruits of total war without the dangers of waging it. But he nevertheless assumed total war as a calculated risk. With the opening of the Spanish Civil War in 1936, all doubts were dispelled. The Spanish war demonstrated the persistence of the will and the means of Europeans to renew total war. It confirmed not only the unprecedented destructiveness of twentieth century warfare but what might be at stake in the outcome of any future European conflict.

The general war which began in 1939, as its predecessor a quarter of a century before, was also to be stalemated. It was similarly escalated—but this time, far beyond the limits of the First World War.

* * *

The coming of the new total warfare was paralleled by a new diplomacy. If the stakes in war become too great—if war can no longer be, in accordance with the Clausewitz dictum, "politics continued by others means"—the reverse tends to be true. Politics becomes war. Distinctions between war and peace break down. The new diplomacy appeared in response to the new total war, both in the fear and in the opportunities created by it.

But even before 1914 something of the new diplomacy was already in evidence in the so-called "armed peace." The danger of general war followed within a few years the consolidation of the German Empire. The existence of a united and powerful German state in the heart of Europe was sufficient to disturb even its creator, Bismarck himself. His "nightmares of coalitions" arose from the fear that other European powers would believe themselves threatened by German hegemony. It was out of this fear of standing alone in some nameless future war that the alliance system was born. Although the Austro-German and Franco-Russian alliances stabilized Europe for a decade after 1894, this same alliance system nevertheless increased the likelihood of general war if war came at all. The mobilization commitments incurred, moreover, made certain that war on a continental scale, even if brief, would produce the most formidable military confrontation on record. Meanwhile, the peacetime absorption in military preparations grew more intense—Europe was being transformed into an armed camp.

With the Russo-Japanese War, the period of comparative stability ended and elements of the new diplomacy appeared. The Russian Revolution of 1905 re-established the possible link between war and revolution—no responsible statesman could now feel completely safe against the perils of domestic upheaval. Moreover, the Russian collapse encouraged a new German aggressiveness that aimed to exploit the weakening of the Franco-Russian partnership. Since the eighteen-nineties the Kaiser's foreign policy had been intermittently aggressive, impelled by romantic dreams of supremacy on both land and sea. But with the Moroccan Crisis of 1905, German policy became characterized by a loudly proclaimed resolution to go to war. It is not likely that Germany's leaders actually sought war. Their expectation was, undoubtedly, that the other side would back down. The German aim was to capitalize on the Franco-Russian weakness and the fear of general war. What Germany practiced was a kind of "cold war" diplomacy.

In the final decade before 1914, as one crisis followed another, the distinction between war and peace progressively broke down. Mounting war hysteria prevented the settlement of major problems on their merits. Each crisis became a test of loyalty that made more rigid the polarization of power. And the conviction that sooner or later war was inevitable became widespread, a factor that undoubtedly helped bring it on. By July, 1914, the distinction between war and peace had, in fact, been obliterated. That was why civilian authorities surrendered so readily to their general staffs. What further facilitated the surrender to the military were the plans for a quick war that placed a premium on rapid mobilization. Hostilities began with the meticulous and irreversible timetables that became operative with the decrees of mobilization. Except for Britain, the actual declarations of war were largely formalities.

Wartime diplomacy paralleled the conduct of the war in its lack of restraint. With the collapse of distinctions between war and peace came the breakdown of distinctions between belligerent and neutral. The German invasion of Belgium and U-boat operations generally had their counterpart in the British blockade and the Anglo-French landings at Salonika. The diplomacy of the Allies was marked by extravagant secret commitments to bolster faltering allies, to gain new ones, or to divide the spoils—the promise of Constantinople to Russia, the secret Treaty of London, and the Sykes-Picot agreement may be cited. The draconic Brest-Litovsk Treaty which Germany imposed on defeated Russia in 1918 was of particular significance. It was an indication of how the war might be resolved elsewhere if Germany were the victor. It was Brest-Litovsk, moreover, that swung Wilson from an aversion to a dictated peace to the acceptance of total victory and unconditional surrender. These policies toward neutral, ally, and enemy alike were not entirely without precedent in European diplomacy. But they were unique from the standpoint of the nineteenth century. And they were pursued with monumental recklessness, as though there would be no postwar reckoning.

The diplomacy of the interwar period was marked by a failure to achieve a "settlement" comparable to that of 1815 and by the danger that a renewal of war meant the renewal of total war. What Trotsky at Brest-Litovsk had called "no war, no peace" now became endemic in Europe. France insisted on maintaining the food blockade for more than a year after the Armistice. Both Germany and Russia were excluded from the Versailles negotiations. Article 231 imposed on Germany the stigma of guilt in perpetuity, while the absence of fixed reparations terms gave an inconclusive character to the entire treaty. The most horrible of wars had been followed by a treaty which was, in many respects, not a treaty of peace, but a prolongation of the war.

Near or real war actually continued in much of Europe for several years. The French reparations policy and the invasion of the Ruhr continued the war "by other means." The Soviet Union, even after the Allied intervention in the Russian civil war, considered herself in a suspended state of war with the bourgeois world. The Russo-Polish War, the Greco-Turkish War, and a variety of internal disorders in Germany, Hungary, and Italy reduced much of Europe to anarchy. Not until Locarno in 1925 was something like peace established in Europe, but still no settlement was reached. To be sure, Germany for the first time was treated as an equal, not as a defeated enemy. But though she accepted her western frontiers, Germany would not make comparable commitments with respect to Poland or Czechoslovakia—nor would the British. Here, and in Eastern Europe generally, there was to be no settlement.

Once embarked on revision of Versailles, Nazi diplomacy employed the fear of total war as its principal weapon. Hitler employed shock tactics, alternating threat and temptation. He may very well have bluffed. German stockpiling of strategic materials and substantial emphasis on munitions production did not begin until 1936. *Wehrmacht* generals, appalled by the risks, were prepared to overthrow him in 1938. But Hitler's methods were effective—the fear of total war was the mainspring of the Anglo-French policy of appeasement. As A. J. P. Taylor has put it, Britain and France "thought that they were faced with the choice between total war and surrender. At first they chose surrender; then they chose total war."[1] Hitler was possibly the first conscious practitioner of modern cold war diplomacy, although pre-1914 precedents must be kept in mind. It is likely that he hoped to attain his goals either without war or by a series of rapid victories. Yet war came in 1939 because Hitler wanted to attain ends for which he was prepared to risk total war.

* * *

Though World War I arose as a problem in the European balance of power system, the defeat of Germany did not lead to its restoration. From its origins in early modern times, the European system had been self-contained. The states of Europe, in the long run, had been able to prevent any of their number from establishing European hegemony. Though the defeat of Germany averted that danger, victory had required the intervention of non-European powers. The end of the European balance of power system was itself of extraordinary importance. But equally significant was the failure of this fact to register clearly during the interwar period.

Even before 1914 there were intimations of an impending transformation of the European balance. European technological advances in transportation and communication—the construction of the Suez and Panama canals, the Trans-Siberian Railway, the introduction of telegraph, telephone, and wireless—had made Europe and the non-European world more responsive to each other's affairs. So, too, had European imperial expansion. Moreover, non-European powers, notably the United States and Japan,

[1] A. J. P. Taylor, *The Origins of the Second World War* (New York, 1961), p. 284.

had by the turn of the century reached the European great-power level. Heretofore, by tradition and circumstance, they had held aloof from European power politics. But their own imperial interests and the new technology now brought closer involvement. The Anglo-Japanese alliance of 1902 and American participation in the negotiations closing the Russo-Japanese War clearly pointed to new departures. Few European statesmen, however, could conceive of a situation which would require a more serious intervention, particularly by the United States, in European affairs. The appearance of a powerful German state was viewed in essentially traditional terms as a European balance of power problem. Germany might have Near Eastern commercial interests and global colonial and naval pretensions, but it was in the real or imagined threat of German hegemony in Europe that Europeans saw the danger of general war. The issues that dominated international politics in Europe on the eve of World War I were all more or less negotiable. What was not negotiable was, in a sense, war itself. Once general war had been permitted to break out, regardless of the immediate occasion, the major issue of such a war would be the German domination of Europe. The alliance system had, in fact, "prepared" for just such a war.

What broke out in 1914 was therefore a European balance-of-power war, but with a difference. The participation from the start of the European overseas empires and the intervention of Britain's ally, Japan, and Germany's ally, Turkey, all combined to extend military and naval operations well beyond Europe. The war became truly a "world war," however, only with American intervention. German victories on the Eastern Front and successes against Britain in the U-boat campaign inevitably forced a reconsideration of traditional American neutrality. American power interests, though not always given adequate emphasis in Wilson's statements, were incompatible with German domination of Europe and the North Atlantic. A German triumph threatened to destroy the very system that had, in part, made possible America's relative aloofness from world politics. The intervention of the United States in 1917 was to be decisive in the defeat of Germany. But the need for American intervention pointed to a fact of utmost importance: German power had outgrown the capacity of the European balance to contain her.

The defeat of Germany concealed the fact that in 1919 her potential for European domination was possibly greater than it had been in 1914. The war, in fact, ended in such a way as to break up the very coalition needed to keep Germany in check. Britain was now suspicious of French designs on the continent. The defeat of both Germany and Russia made possible the political fragmentation of much of Central and Eastern Europe. The United States failed to support a Rhineland guarantee, as did Britain, and withdrew into isolation. The Soviet Union and the Western powers viewed each other with mutual distrust and hostility. But Versailles had created in Germany a fierce resentment without breaking her power, and her industry and unity had survived the war intact. German impotence would merely be temporary: only an alliance of Britain, France, the United States, and the Soviet Union could defend the treaties against her.

In these circumstances, the French made their own arrangements, based on what appeared usable in the wreckage produced by the war. Germany was denied an equality which would, in fact, have given her European supremacy; Russia was to be kept out of Europe altogether. The allies of France, the lesser states of Central and East-Central Europe, became the key to the French system of security. Their assigned role was the encirclement of Germany and the containment of the Soviet Union—a dual responsibility that was beyond their means.

Both Germany and the Soviet Union were revisionist, and the French system could work only as long as Germany and Russia remained prostrate. Moreover, the British undermined the system from the start. As early as December, 1921, Lloyd George indicated that Britain regarded Germany as a bulwark against the Soviets and was not much interested in Germany's eastern frontiers. Also, on the basis of the Locarno treaties, Germany was entitled to believe that Britain considered a revision of Versailles a possibility in the east.

With the blatantly revisionist Nazis in power, the problem of German containment took an ominous turn. The German occupation of the Rhineland in 1936 was the first step in the breakdown of the French system of security. British failure to back France was responsible for French appeasement, but American failure to back Britain was "a more distant and basic reason." The Czech crisis of 1938 raised the possibility of Soviet inclusion in an Anglo-French balance against the Nazis. Such participation, however, was bound to open the question of Soviet revisionism. The Soviets, without common frontiers, could neither aid the Czechs nor attack Germany. But at Munich the Anglo-French alliance opted in favor of German revision and turned over to Germany the role of bulwark against the Soviets. It was Munich that probably convinced Stalin that his choice now lay between a deal with Hitler or war. By the Nazi-Soviet Pact, recalling both prewar and postwar collaboration between Germany and Russia, the buffers between them were removed. Both Versailles and Brest-Litovsk were now liquidated.

In World War II, however, Hitler repeated Ludendorff's blunder. He erred in attacking the Soviets, not so much in miscalculating Soviet strength, as in freeing Japan from the danger of a Siberian war. The result was the gigantic Japanese gamble of Pearl Harbor which again brought the United States into a European war. Again the war became global and again an extra-European coalition was necessary to put down Germany. The second war confirmed the first in Germany's failure to establish European hegemony and in the eclipse of the European balance of power system.

* * *

The decline of the European system was paralleled by the emergence of a successor, epitomized in "Wilson vs. Lenin." However, the political and ideological implications of this first confrontation of the "superpowers," only briefly delineated in the closing stages of the war, were by no means clear. Herein lies the root of an extraordinary failure in statesmanship during the interwar period.

The notion of a Europe someday overshadowed by superpowers—the young American giant or the Russian colossus—was by no means novel before 1914. European statesmen, however, took little account of the possibility. American power, though not unrecognized, seemed distant, and Russian potential was believed enormous, though plagued by serious weaknesses. Equally remote before 1914 was the possibility that ideology might play a role of any considerable importance in international politics. Although the intellectual climate of prewar Europe did become increasingly ideological, diplomacy continued to demonstrate an overriding concern with *Realpolitik*—that republican France and tsarist Russia could join in alliance in 1894 was symptomatic. No European nation identified itself explicitly in international politics with an ideological system. All believed themselves to be on a more or less common course of material and spiritual advance. Moreover, for Europeans to look abroad for material aid or ideological inspiration would have been considered an absurdity. The American republic was viewed as a frontier appendage of the European world. Russia, too, was thought European, though backward.

World War I favored both the rise of the superpowers and the triumph of ideologies. That the war increasingly took on the quality of an ideological crusade was due to the requirements of morale both on the home and the battle fronts. No clear ideological division, however, was possible until the fall of tsarism and the almost simultaneous intervention of the United States. Then, in 1917, the division between "Allied democracy" and German *Kultur* crystallized.

A further differentiation followed the Bolshevik Revolution in November. Wilson and Lenin appeared almost simultaneously as rival prophets of a new postwar order. Wilson's Fourteen Points of January, 1918, were announced in anticipation of Lenin's Twenty-one Theses for Peace presented later, in February. Both pronouncements were calls of "outsiders" who, in a sense, condemned all belligerents and rejected the very system that had made the war possible. Wilson's idealism bore the mark of traditional American aloofness from world politics. Lenin rejected the entire system of "bourgeois" institutions and values—an act of rebellion against the European order. Both addressed the masses and called for the transformation of the war into a revolutionary crusade: Wilson for national self-determination and democracy, and Lenin for "world revolution" and a "classless society." Both demanded a warless world and supranational organizations: the League of Nations for Wilson, the Communist International for Lenin.

What gave force and relevance to both appeals was power. The United States emerged at the war's conclusion by far the single most formidable financial and industrial nation in the world. In the margin of American preponderance and in its dramatic appearance on the world scene there were elements of the "revolutionary." But the Soviet Union, if it survived, would also represent a revolutionary kind of power. The Bolshevik Revolution had transformed old Russia from the tail end of Europe and the most retarded and reactionary of its great powers into the leader of a worldwide anti-European revolt.

The war had given birth to the superpowers, but neither was willing to assume responsibilities for the stability of postwar Europe; the rise of the superpowers was, therefore, to have disastrous consequences. The United States, briefly, could have assumed world leadership, for a vast number of the world's people were still moved by America as the land of both abundance and freedom. But the United States had never been in touch with them, and the idealism that had briefly made Americans eager to save the world now made them turn away from Europe. Americans feared being sucked into the European power game. That United States interests and responsibilities had been drastically altered by the war failed to register on the American mind. With the refusal to guarantee the Rhineland, to ratify the Versailles Treaty, or to join the League of Nations, the United States "withdrew" from Europe and tossed aside the fruits of victory.

But American isolationism was initially political—it could not be economic. The economic ties created by the war were closer than anyone suspected—the Allies had needed United States aid to win the war; now all of Europe needed her aid to recover from it. There was nothing in this novel relationship that made the Great Depression inevitable, and yet the main features of the collapse can be traced to it. The frenzy of overproduction and overspeculation in the United States during the twenties is traceable to the tremendous stimulus of wartime growth. So too, the United States position as universal creditor was brought about by the war and reinforced by American financial support of European and especially German recovery. It was the Wall Street crash of 1929 that brought the flow of credit to an abrupt halt and pulled the props from under Europe's postwar economic recovery.

To the political isolationism of the twenties was now added the economic isolationism of the thirties. American attempts to deal with the collapse were based on the methods of autarky introduced during the war. The Smoot-Hawley Tariff of 1930, the "torpedoing" of the World Economic Conference in 1933, and the domestic legislation of the New Deal generally blocked all efforts to deal with the Depression on an international basis. Even the dangers to world peace after 1933 failed to evoke any greater sense of American responsibility. American sympathies were clear enough: Americans gave "moral support" to resistance to Hitler. But the strength of the United States regular army in 1939 was less than 200,000. As A. J. P. Taylor has indicated, "resolute isolationism" would have held Britain and France from war. Resolute support might have stopped Hitler.

In contrast with the United States, the Soviet Union wanted world leadership but could not get it. Capitalizing on the domestic unrest that followed World War I, the new Communist parties, aided and abetted by Moscow, spread rapidly in Europe among the alienated and disillusioned on all intellectual and social levels. Moreover, the Red Army took the offensive. But the thrust into the heart of Europe was blocked by the collapse of "Soviet" republics in Bavaria and Hungary and the defeat of the Red Army before Warsaw in August, 1920. The Soviet regime now also "withdrew" from Europe. Soviet isolationism was by no means imposed from without by the establishment of the *Cordon Sanitaire*. By turning to revolutionary Marxism, the new Russia broke with the solidarity of the European order. In official theory, fortified by resentments engendered by the revolution and intervention, the Soviets were in a suspended state of war with

Europe. Furthermore, internal problems dictated extreme caution. The Soviet Union was revisionist—the territorial losses of Brest-Litovsk had not been entirely recovered. But Europe was an area of high risk.

Notwithstanding her isolationism, Soviet-inspired communism continued to pursue the phantom of world revolution through propaganda and agitation. The result in Europe was to further domestic discord and debility. Communism claimed to be the heir of prewar proletarian revolutionism: The assertion of this claim against socialism hopelessly split and poisoned the proletarian movement everywhere. The destruction of working-class unity paralyzed the left more than once during the interwar years. Where the "red menace" seriously threatened—as in Bavaria, Hungary, and Italy—its worst consequence was the stampede to fascism which it engendered. This is not to say that fascism was pure anti-communism; but fear of the "reds" provided fascism with opportunities to reach not only the influential few but important elements among the masses. The Soviets failed to see in fascism, until too late, the threat to their own interests. Marxist ideology gave assurance that only a proletarian revolution was possible. The Communist attack was therefore directed against the liberal bourgeois regime and its socialist collaborators. Fascism was viewed as the extreme form of bourgeois rule and as a preliminary to the proletarian revolution.

That the road to a "Soviet Germany" lay through a Nazi Germany was a miscalculation, however, which later cost the Soviets dearly. Not until 1935 did Stalin show awareness of the dangers inherent in the policies pursued by Communist parties in Europe. Only then was the party line favoring the formation of antifascist "popular fronts," of communists, socialists, and liberals, formulated. Only then did the Soviets press for "collective security." But it was too late. Almost two decades of Soviet subversion in

Europe had created profound distrust. The triumph of the Popular Front in France and the outbreak of the Spanish Civil War in 1936, in fact, raised renewed fears of communism among conservatives in both Britain and France. It was then that the appeasement policy crystallized. Though rooted in fear of total war, the ideological implications of appeasement now became anti-Communist. The Nazi-Soviet Pact and, indeed, the outbreak of war in 1939 were the fruits of the failure of a Soviet-Western accommodation—a failure that had its roots in the Soviet pursuit of its revolutionary mission.

The war of 1939, however, was to take an unexpected turn: By the end of 1941, both the Soviet Union and the United States were allies against Germany; both decided the outcome of the war in 1945. And once more they assumed roles taken up briefly at the conclusion of the First World War.

* * *

The revolt against Europe, particularly by aroused Asiatics, was not only powerfully reinforced by the war but given new directions. Heretofore, one European power had succeeded another in establishing colonial preponderance. But the colonial world had remained a European preserve. World War I worked to continue the succession, but now largely at the expense of Europeans.

The rebellion against European colonialism goes back possibly to the Sepoy Mutiny of 1857, but continuity is marked only after the Boxer Rebellion of 1900 and the Japanese victory over Russia in 1905. It was, in fact, the Japanese who first gave clear orientation to the revolt. Japan's Westernization late in the nineteenth century had been undertaken largely to prevent European domination. When Japan defeated Russia, the entire non-European world was electrified. The Japanese had defeated a white imperialist European power. Subject peoples everywhere now concluded that the adoption of European science, industry, and organization was essential to emancipation. The leadership of nationalist movements in Asia was composed largely of a native intelligentsia "apprenticed" in Europe, and for the most part, devoted to a nationalism that was militantly liberal and democratic. Such native revolutionary movements swept through Persia in 1906, Turkey in 1908, and China in 1912.

But another stimulus to unrest came from Europeans. European powers were not above undermining each other's colonialism, and indirectly, European colonialism generally. Germany was particularly active in fomenting anti-British agitation in South Africa, Egypt, and India and anti-French sentiments in North Africa. Italy, too, railed against Anglo-French imperialism; Italian nationalists drew novel distinctions between "plutocratic" imperialist powers and their own "proletarian" Italy, between the "have" and "have not" nations. Until 1914, however, the European position abroad still seemed safe. Europeans stood in a relation to the rest of mankind never before achieved. And they assumed, quite naturally, that it would last indefinitely.

The war sharpened the colonial problem and gave it a new turn. Almost all Asiatic peoples were involved. India, China, and Japan were, formally at least, aligned with the "democracies" against "autocracy and militarism." But with the exception of Japan, they were all in colonial or semicolonial status with respect to Western powers or to Japan. Though largely isolated from military conflict, they could not be isolated from the hopes and expectations raised by the war. The colonial peoples were stirred by Wilson's call "to make the world safe for democracy." Home governments, to avoid colonial difficulties, made concessions, but they were reluctant to go very far. The principle of self-determination, if carried to its logical conclusion, could only mean the liquidation of colonialism.

The Bolshevik Revolution, however, opened an alternative path to liberation. For Asians, the Russian Revolution had great relevance. Old Russia, though herself imperialist, had also been the object of European imperialism. Moreover, the relationship in Marxist ideology between capitalism and imperialism seemed obvious to colonial peoples—both were foreign. The new Russian regime, therefore, could effectively exploit the frustrated ambitions of the native intelligentsia by fusing revolutionary socialism with the developing anti-European revolt. In linking the Communist revolt within Europe to the anti-European revolt without, Lenin made a bid for global leadership. Wilsonism and Leninism, therefore, became competing systems not only within Europe but outside.

But the Japanese were to be the principal beneficiaries of a war in which European states seemed bent on mutual destruction. The Japanese seized Shantung and occupied Germany's Pacific islands; the Chinese took over the territorial concessions of Germany and Austria and stopped the Boxer payments. The solid front of European colonialism, which had already shown signs of cracking, was now broken. The Japanese, moreover, attempted to impose the Twenty-one Demands on China. Had they succeeded, China would have been transformed into a Japanese protectorate. In any case, while Europeans fought, Japan established her preeminence among foreigners in Peking and intervened in Siberia. Her industrial growth and expanded markets increasingly threatened the European position in Asia.

The hold of European colonialism and imperialism was clearly weakened by the war. The temporary enlargement of the British and French empires was deceptive: Acceptance of the League mandate system in the Near East and elsewhere implied the passing of the colonial age. Restrictions were placed on the rule of colonial peoples, eventual self-government was promised for the most advanced, and exploitation of one people by another was declared morally wrong. In the Far East, moreover, the anti-European movement had been heightened by the war. The Chinese had been hopeful at Versailles, but they were so enraged at the confirmation of the Japanese seizure of Shantung that they refused to sign the treaty. The European powers lost a golden opportunity to steer Chinese nationalism into pro-Western channels. Anti-imperialism in China now became more clearly anti-European as well as anti-Japanese. As Western influences waned, a Communist Party emerged, while the republic itself was swept away, to be succeeded by a host of military adventurers. Japan also had serious grievances against Europe—she had, in fact, threatened not to sign the Versailles treaty or to join the League. The Japanese believed their war acquisitions inadequate. Though admitted to the Big Five, they failed to obtain acceptance of the principle of racial equality in the Covenant. The latter particularly hurt their pride. The humiliation was aggravated by United States and Dominion immigration restrictions based on race. The war, therefore, not only heightened anti-European sentiment but engendered a counter-imperialism which drew strength from anti-Europeanism.

The Soviets were first in attempting to exploit this opportunity. Their failure at world revolution in Europe inspired a "flanking maneuver" in Asia, where Europe seemed more vulnerable. By supporting nationalism and by allying with nonproletarian groups, they demonstrated far greater tactical ingenuity in promoting the colonial struggle in Asia than the class struggle in Europe. The Soviets, moreover, had effective selling points. In the twenties they represented the overthrow of imperialism. In the thirties they pointed to their "economic miracle"—in one stupendous leap they had transformed the primitive economy which they had inherited into an industrial giant. The Soviet offensive, however, was destined to be premature. Communism in China ended in a fiasco in the twenties, while in India competition from liberal elements remained vigorous. In any case, Soviet internal problems and the danger of war in Europe dictated caution in Asia.

Japan, though, was far better situated to capitalize on the consequences of the war. Her own resentment against Europe was strong and she could exploit the resentment of others. She also possessed the military power and the proximity to the coveted territories. During the twenties, liberal European influences weakened as the government gave way to Shinto and military elements hostile to Europe and the United States and bent on further expansion. In 1931, the Japanese began their undeclared war against China in Manchuria. The League of Nations, in the first test involving a great power, failed to give security to a member state. Japan's defiance was a serious blow to the prestige of the League, in Europe as well as in Asia. As aggression spread to Europe, the Japanese planned the creation of an East Asian "Co-prosperity Sphere," extending from Manchuria to Southeast Asia, and hoped to draw strength from anti-Europeanism throughout Asia. If their leadership were accepted, Japan promised to organize "Asia for the Asiatics." Many suspected it would be Asia for the Japanese. Japan waited for war to break out in Europe once again to give her a free hand. While the Soviet Union was fighting for its life in 1941, Japan finally struck at Pearl Harbor. The first phase of the anti-European revolt now came to a climax with the Japanese conquests in Asia and the Pacific. The old European colonial system, weakened everywhere by the First World War, collapsed in Asia with the second.

* * *

The revolt against Europe was paralleled by the rise of "global" history. True global history, the continuing interaction of one part of the world on another, is comparatively recent. World War I both hastened and gave shape to this development.

The outlines of an emerging global history were already in evidence in the nineteenth century. Until then the great segments of mankind lived largely apart, separated not only by great distances but by their cultures. European colonialism brought them together. European empire-building in Asia, Africa, and the island territories forged the ties between mother country and colony. European transportation and communication facilities drew non-Europeans closer to Europe. European finance and industry fashioned a European-centered world economy. European education brought a native elite into the orbit of European culture.

But the vastly expanded ties with Europe were often on terms that were degrading and humiliating to non-Europeans. In the final decades before the war, as E. H. Carr has pointed out, the demand for equality among Europeans passed over from a question of classes to one of nations. And the struggle between the "haves" and the "have nots" became indistinguishable from the struggle for predominance. Moreover, this demand for equality, in turn, passed over from Europe to the nations of the world.

Events in the Far East between 1895 and 1905 already pointed in this direction. The Japanese victory over China, the United States retention of the Philippines after the Spanish-American War, the Anglo-Japanese alliance, and the Japanese victory of 1905 marked the rise of two new claimants, the United States and Japan, to great power status. The Russo-Japanese War, in fact, may be regarded as the first global crisis, involving the European, Asian, and American continents. The shell that enclosed Europe's preeminence had only to be shattered.

World War I, though fought largely in Europe, was really a vast global enterprise—Europe became an enormous cauldron into which men and resources from Asia, Africa, and America were poured. The loss in blood and treasure, however, worked to reduce Europe's preeminence. Casualties and physical destruction in Europe were without precedent—no one can say how much genius and talent were interred in the mass graves. Britain, moreover, lost a quarter of its investments abroad, the French a third, and the Germans all. Industrialization was speeded up in the non-European parts of the world, and vast European markets abroad were lost.

From the war there also emerged two global secular ideologies. Both implied, if not a lowering of Europe's status, then an elevation of non-Europeans more nearly to the European level. Wilson's ideal was one of a world order of equal, sovereign states; Lenin preached the doctrine of world revolution against European capitalist domination. Neither represented tendencies that were entirely new. The World Court and the Hague Peace Conferences, on one hand, and the various prewar "internationals" (socialist, syndicalist, and anarchist), on the other, were symptomatic. But the war now gave a new ideological and institutional relevance to global tendencies.

Global tendencies were the product of an extended evolution, but the new global institutions emerged more directly out of the war—and they passed on to the postwar world problems created by the war. The initial composition of the League was a reflection of the way the war had been fought and concluded. Germany was not admitted until 1926, and the Soviets not until 1934. The United States never joined. Then also, the very principle on which the League operated, national self-determination, had been formulated as a weapon of ideological warfare. When it came to full implementation, however, the Allies had balked. The League therefore became the scene of continuing complaints by minorities—the new states were sometimes more intolerant than their predecessors. Moreover, the League had been the creation of a few victorious European states. With some justice, one could see in the League an essentially European institution; one could also see it as an institution created by the victors to maintain the status quo.

And yet, something of Wilson's vision was at least partially realized: For the first time peoples of the entire globe—the powerful and the weak, the new and the old, people of all tongues and dress—met in a common assembly. No longer could the fate of major portions of the globe be determined exclusively by the representatives of a half-dozen major European states. Although the weaknesses of the League were recognized, the belief persisted in many quarters that, given both the time and the will, it might develop into an effective instrument of world peace. Even inequities in the peace treaties could be peacefully resolved at a later date.

That the League was to collapse was due not only to inherent weaknesses derived from the war but also to the appearance of "anti-Leagues" with similar global pretensions. The Comintern drew strength from all lands among those alienated and frustrated by the war and the false hopes it had raised. But the Comintern was a rather obvious instrument of Soviet foreign policy and communism failed to conquer permanent ground anywhere outside the Soviet Union. The Rome-Berlin-Tokyo Axis, like the Comintern, had its roots in the war. The German-Italian Pact of 1936, to which Japan formally adhered in 1940, was, substantially, a revisionist anti-League. But it was not a true global system—the Axis was a series of improvised alliances without common plans except the destruction of the League and the Versailles arrangements. Japan's aggression in 1931, however, was the beginning of the end for the League. After Italy's invasion of Abyssinia in 1935, its authority was spent, and Nazi aggression brought about the final collapse. The fall of the League was attended by a total loss of faith in the sanctity of treaties: By the end of the thirties, states no longer kept promises, nor could they even be expected to defend their own interests coherently.

The collapse of the first attempt to establish a global order was followed by a second global war. And out of the ruins of the second war arose a successor to the defunct League. In many ways, the United Nations, with more awesome responsibilities, was to be only a slightly improved version of its predecessor.

II

In European values and institutions, World War I also inspired a profound transformation. "Total war" designates with equal effectiveness not only the way in which the enemy was fought in the field, but also the kind of mobilization required on the home front. In the new war-making functions of the state were to be found the most powerful engines of domestic change. The impact of the war, however, could not be everywhere the same, because the nature of the war experience varied from nation to nation, as did the role of tradition and the force of circumstance. As a turning point on the domestic scene, therefore, the war worked a wide range of consequences.

* * *

The war fortified and spread an intellectual revolt already under way against the standards of the nineteenth century. But where in postwar Europe a modicum of domestic stability could be maintained, the new ideas were confined to intellectual and artistic circles or found lodgement among extremist political groups that remained marginal.

Late nineteenth-century science and scholarship, reinforcing the earlier assault of Romanticism, had already begun to undermine the fundamental values of the age. These were rooted largely in the assumptions of the Enlightenment—that the universe is a harmony operating in accord with natural law; that man is capable of the free use of reason; and that reason is an adequate instrument in understanding and mastering the universe. But the new view of the physical universe that emerged from Einsteinian relativity, of nature that derived from Darwinian evolutionism, or of man himself implied in the work of Pavlov and Freud drained much of the meaning from the accepted absolutes. From about the eighteen-nineties the new science and scholarship fostered rebellion not only in philosophy, literature and art, but also in political thought and movements. Characteristic of the latter was the discovery of mass politics and the role of the irrational in moving the masses. A new value was placed on the role of myth, elites, and will to power. The new currents were in evidence throughout Europe and in a variety of movements—anarchist, syndicalist, racist, nationalist, and imperialist. These groups reviled the "decadence" of European values and institutions and proclaimed the urgency of a politico-spiritual conquest on an apocalyptic scale. But until 1914 there was little indication that apocalyptic ideologies, though widely circulated, extended much beyond minority groups. Certainly, the statesmen who went to war in 1914 wanted to preserve the status quo.

In removing the restraints of civilized life, the war seemed to confirm something of the prewar intellectual and political currents of irrationalism. The war itself was, for Europeans, an irrational happening, though conducted with the most advanced technology. Brutalities that Europeans had previously inflicted only on the uncivilized were now inflicted on each other. Society seemed at the mercy of blind, demonic forces. But the passions aroused by the war revealed the extraordinary energies in the masses available for collective purposes. These energies were "mobilized"—that is, organized, cultivated and directed. Elie Halévy has called this aspect of the war the "mobilization of enthusiasm," but it could with equal justice have been called the "mobilization of hatred." In the "social engineering" employed to sustain morale, in any case, is to be found the first modern effort at systematic, nationwide manipulation of collective passions. The American intervention and the Bolshevik Revolution, moreover, gave the myth-makers their supreme opportunity—they made the war "ideological." Wilson and Lenin reached out over the heads of state to the masses the world over. In the final years of the war, their summons to those masses was to fight for the millennium.

Even regimes that "won the war" experienced no full "recovery" from the intellectual and emotional orgy that had accompanied it. In Britain and France, though Italy was a notable exception, victory had reaffirmed the legitimacy of regimes in the eyes of the masses. Tradition and circumstances, therefore, favored the restoration in the masses of something of the ideals and practices of the prewar era. But even here, for an intellectual elite, the war had eroded further the prewar verities, an erosion that had become clear even as the war had progressed. "All the great words," wrote D. H. Lawrence, "were cancelled out for that generation." [2] Yet disillusionment with nineteenth-century standards, even intellectual rebellion against them, had only limited political consequences. Philosophical, literary, and artistic movements might be tormented

[2] Quoted in Barbara Tuchman, *The Guns of August* (New York, 1962), p. 489.

by doubts or outbursts of nihilism, but political movements that aimed at drastic political overturn remained peripheral or weak. With the coming of the Depression and the triumph of Hitler, however, the distress of the early twenties returned. In Western Europe new converts were won to intellectual despair or revolt, while subversive movements expanded rapidly. Only emergency measures and the hold of tradition prevented complete demoralization—France, nevertheless, came close to it. Elsewhere, the *terribles simplificateurs*, whose coming had been foreseen by the historian Jacob Burckhardt, signaled the real triumph of the irrational.

* * *

The extreme expression of the intellectual revolt was the rise of a cult of violence. Here, too, the roots were prewar. But where the war ended in defeat or breakdown, peacetime restraints were removed and violence was provided with a mass basis.

The roots of the modern cult of violence are to be found in nineteenth-century romantic nihilism. Its beginning, Camus has written, was in Dostoevsky's statement: "If nothing is true, everything is permitted." [3] The words are those of the Devil speaking to Ivan Karamazov. If there is no God, if there is no standard outside history by which actions can be judged, then even murder is permitted.

What began as a literary movement, however, received apparent support from other sources. Movements of social protest and national unification in the nineteenth century, it could be said, had been movements of revolution and war. Darwinian biology, moreover, seemed to give scientific support to the idea that in history, too, struggle and violence might be considered desirable. A dramatic manifestation of the cult of violence came in

[3] Albert Camus, *The Rebel*, translated by Anthony Bower (New York, 1957), p. 57.

the series of spectacular assassinations by anarchists at the end of the century—Alexander II, McKinley, Humbert, Elizabeth of Austria. By the turn of the century, the cult had found its theoretician in Sorel. It was the anarchists, he wrote, who taught revolutionaries not to be ashamed of acts of violence. Violence, when a clear expression of a movement with a mission, was "sublime" and no apologies need be made for it.

From the end of the nineteenth century to World War I, Europe abounded in movements that glorified the virtues of violence, from revolutionary syndicalism and Marxism to integral nationalism and imperialism. Events in 1905 gave a kind of relevance to the cult with the first major war and the first major revolutionary disturbance in Europe since 1871. Extremists on all sides, wrote Croce, contaminated the air that Europeans breathed:

> Warfare, bloodshed, slaughter, harshness, cruelty, were no longer objects of deprecation and repugnance, . . . but were regarded as necessities for the ends to be achieved and as acceptable and desirable. . . .[4]

Nevertheless, on the eve of 1914 the vast majority of Europeans still appeared to have faith in the virtues of international and domestic peace. Even the cult of violence, though there were exceptions, was more literary and esthetic than explicitly political.

What the war did was to make violence on a massive, all-inclusive scale an everyday occurrence. Among combatants alone there were some 10 million dead and over 21 million wounded. To kill or to expect a violent end became a commonplace in the daily lives of millions of young men. But the physical violence of the battlefield had its counterpart in the violence to the mind. Only an inflamed public opinion could sustain men and women in

[4] Benedetto Croce, *History of Europe in the Nineteenth Century*, translated by Henry Furst (New York, 1963), p. 341.

the awesome struggle. In giving way to an orgy of destruction, however, an entire generation of young men had been educated in little else—and what began as "war" in 1914 ended in "revolution" in 1917–18.

The cult of violence persisted in vigor and became more explicitly political in those parts of Europe where the war had ended in near or complete collapse of prewar institutions. The new Soviet regime was, of course, in the midst of revolutionary upheaval. As Marxists, its leaders had "reasons" for their violence. The official organ of the Cheka declared in 1919:

> All is permitted for us, for we are the first in the world to draw the sword not in behalf of enslavement and oppression but for the sake of freedom and emancipation from servitude.[5]

But in Germany, Italy, Hungary, and elsewhere in East-Central Europe, the effect of the war was also to prolong violence into the postwar years. Resentment against civilians who had "lost the war," opposition to the peace treaties, fear of communism—all this sharpened by postwar unemployment—vastly increased the number of extremists. Many were veterans organized in such groups as the German Free Corps or the Italian Fascists. Intellectually, these groups had prewar roots. But the war experience of these young men and the situation to which they returned worked to transform them into bands of armed and uniformed ruffians. Private armies—fascist, revisionist, even bands that professed no ideology—were rampant in the early twenties. Their adherents "yearned for the chaotic and virile hell" of the trenches. What there had been of the literary or esthetic in prewar violence now quickly degenerated into a vulgar and brutal gangsterism. The goals of these groups, if they had any, were based essentially on the ideology of war propaganda. The "new order"

[5] Quoted in Bertram D. Wolfe, *Marxism* (New York, 1965), p. 368.

which they promised was to be based on combat. Formal doctrine, however, meant little to them. Italian Fascism was originally revolutionary and republican. But the movement was transformed into a political party that accommodated itself to the monarchy without in the least giving up its violence. What Mussolini demonstrated was a new technique in the use of violence—how power could be taken while preserving the appearance of legality.

The cult of violence received new strength in the thirties with the enlargement and proliferation of extremist movements; the totalitarian and pseudototalitarian regimes of the era gave violence official doctrinal sanction. The Soviet regime preached "class war," and though it condemned traditional "national war" as bourgeois, it considered the renewal of war with the capitalist states as someday inevitable. In any case, out of the moral code in which "all is permitted" came the liquidation of the kulaks as a class, forced collectivization, labor camps, party purges, and the Moscow trials. The same was substantially true of Italian Fascism and especially of German Nazism. War was noble, and love of peace a mark of decadence. This ethical system was the basis of a foreign policy whose only apparent instrument was violence or the threat of violence. For Germany the cult of violence led to ruthless elimination of political opposition, unprecedented concentration camp cruelties, and the "final solution" of the Jewish question.

* * *

The war profoundly influenced the general character of European economic development; even where the war or its aftermath resulted in no marked change in regime, it gave new impetus to a transformation of the system of capitalism already under way.

The European economic system before the war was one of substantially free enterprise capitalism: extreme mobility of goods, global specialization, and general acceptance of the gold standard. But the severe economic crisis of 1873, which began in the United States, revealed the dangers of a largely uncontrolled business cycle. The rapid growth of corporate business, the increasing demand for labor and social legislation, and the rising clamor for tariff protection (by both capital and labor) were all largely responses to the hazards of economic exposure. By the turn of the century a clear trend toward national or neomercantile systems was in evidence everywhere on the Continent. The pacesetter was Germany, whose economy was tightly welded through a series of trusts and cartels and, above all, through her great banking establishments. Britain and her empire were alone in their strict adherence to free trade. And yet, the period 1880 to 1914 was still one of a substantially unregulated capitalism. Business was still relatively free from governmental control. To be sure, there was cause for alarm in the maldistribution of wealth and in the size of the gap between the most industrially advanced and the most backward; but economic growth was almost everywhere evident, and the system of capitalism seemed in no great danger.

The war weakened the older capitalism. No one had foreseen that a war economy might differ from one of peace; no one had anticipated the kind of industrial mobilization that would be required. By 1916, however, the war had become one of national survival—what would have been rejected in peacetime even on the grounds of social justice or economic efficiency was readily accepted as a war measure. All belligerents were obliged to make a reality the notion of economic management. Such management required a system of boards or bureaus that planned, coordinated, and controlled both manpower and resources on a national and even transnational scale. But in a variety of ways the resulting economic strain or dislocation also undermined the prewar system: Russian mobilization was hopelessly inadequate and collapsed in discredit. Elsewhere on the Continent, the preoccupation with war manufactures meant speeding up industrial growth in prewar European markets overseas or their loss to the United States or Japan. The American economy, however, in attempting to meet domestic, Allied and foreign demands generally, responded with such vigor to the wartime mobilization that by war's end the productive capacity of the United States (which even in 1914 was first in the world) had outstripped by far all other nations. The very successes of the mobilization, however, also served to call into question the merits of the prewar system of capitalism.

The experience in dealing with the wartime economic and industrial crisis was not to be forgotten. To be sure, the desire to return to economic "normalcy" was so intense that there was little inclination, with the notable exception of the Soviet Union, to continue to employ the new techniques of national economic management. European nations were intent on dismantling their militarized economies. At Paris, moreover, no plans were made for the rehabilitation of the world economy, and the discussion of the inter-Allied debt was excluded. The close connection between reparations and debts and their relation to the world economy was not foreseen. Instead, it became the goal of the United States to restore the foundations of prewar capitalism. Though the postwar slump and mass unemployment gave currency to the ideas of the new Keynesian economics—government manipulation of the economy to ensure both stability and growth—these were not heeded. And the large-scale American lending abroad, in any case, at first appeared successful. The crash of 1929 and the ensuing depression, however, brought American lending and European recovery to an abrupt and catastrophic end. Yet, as previously indicated, if the war had helped bring on the Depression, the war had also provided a model for dealing with it. The autarkic methods devised during those years were now adapted to meet the ravages of declining production, unemployment, and social insecurity. The world economy and what remained of the older capitalism were struck down not only by the Depression, but by the measures employed to cure it. Though the Depression began as an American crisis that spread across the Atlantic, its lessons were more fully taken to heart and conclusively accepted in the shattered economies of Europe. Here came the final rejection of prewar unregulated capitalism.

* * *

A more drastic rejection of prewar capitalism, though varied, came from revolutionary currents intensified and modified by the war experience. Where World War I ended in defeat or breakdown, prewar revolutionary movements of nationalism and socialism seized their opportunity. But the war, by bringing about the "socialization" of nationalism and the "nationalization" of socialism, also determined the character of postwar revolutionary movements and regimes.

Nationalism and socialism had been well established in the late nineteenth century in their opposition to liberal capitalism. The two currents, however, long seemed sharply separated not only by the social composition of their adherents, but by their doctrines. Revolutionary nationalism had tended to ignore the coming of modern industry and was contemptuous of the masses. Revolutionary socialism viewed the nation-state as a "bourgeois" creation and proclaimed a fervent internationalism. Yet the extremes possessed a number of common traits. Both were based on assumptions of "bourgeois decadence." At heart, socialists could be patriotic, while many extreme nationalists were social radicals and collectivists. Prewar efforts to bridge the gap between nationalism and socialism were not without some success. Extremist groups in France and Italy, notably those segments of revolutionary syndicalism and integral nationalism under the influence of Sorel, explored the possibilities of both doctrinal and organizational merger. But the tendency in France was confined to a few intellectuals, and, in Italy, to marginal groups. In Germany and Austria, efforts to merge nationalism and socialism were facilitated by antisemitic propaganda. Traditional Christian Jew-hatred was deeply rooted and easily manipulated: The Jew could be depicted readily as either the national or social enemy, as either radical or capitalist. Though the national-social ferment was marginal, it was nevertheless symptomatic of a protofascism—a tendency to transcend on a revolutionary plane the traditional nineteenth-century political categories of right and left.

The war mobilization created something of the very regimes desired by prewar extremists. At the start, both nationalists and socialists, for their own reasons and with minor exceptions, found that they could support the war. Nationalist groups saw in the war a renewal of the national consciousness weakened by the industrial struggles of the nineteenth century. With few exceptions, socialists abandoned class for national resentments and rallied to the fatherland—the only antiwar group among them was the Russian Bolshevik leadership, for the most part in exile.

But all extremist groups, from nationalists who fervently supported the war to the bitter end to those socialists who came to detest it as a bloody bourgeois venture, were convinced that the war would lead to revolutionary departures. Nationalists recognized that modern war was an affair of all social categories and that national resources required mobilization regardless of property rights. Socialists saw in mobilization their collectivist ideas —planning, direction, compulsion, taxation—put into practice in the national interest. If "national socialism" can be defined as the organization of collective existence within a national system, then Germany in 1917 was the first to enter the era of national socialisms. Her need was greater because of the blockade. Moreover, the basis for such an economy already existed and the military tradition favored its operation. Rathenau, who was chiefly responsible for creating the German system, was well aware of its significance:

> In its methods, it is closely akin to communism and yet it departs essentially from the prophecies and demands resulting from radical theories . . . Our methods will leave their impression on future times.[6]

The German experience was appropriately labeled *Kriegswirtschaft* (war economy) or *Kriegssozialismus* (war socialism). It was now available as a model. It could be employed by those who aimed to destroy or modify the prewar economic order and replace it with one based more clearly on rationalization, standardization, and mass production—on national and collective interests before individual interests.

The war had not only heightened nationalist sentiment but seemed to reaffirm the viability of the nation-state. In the postwar accommodation of revolutionary nationalism and socialism, nationalism everywhere took precedence.

The Soviet regime was, almost from the very outset, "statist." The Bolsheviks who made the revolution may very well have been "internationalists," but whatever their intentions, the failure of world revolution and the press of internal problems required the reestablishment of the apparatus of the state in both foreign and domestic affairs. The statist character of the regime was only partially camouflaged by a federal organization and a claim to leadership of an international movement. Federalism was a

[6] Quoted in Koppel S. Pinson, *Modern Germany* (New York, 1954), p. 323.

façade for a rigidly centralized autocracy, with no federalism where it really mattered—in the party. And the Third International, dominated by Moscow, was even less of an "international" than the second. Moreover, the initiation of the Five-Year Plan imposed an autarky on the Soviet economy, advancing further the process of centralization under state control. Conceivably, the Soviets could have had planned industrialization and collectivization without the benefit of the national war mobilizations. But the fact is that Lenin, and Russian Marxists generally, had studied the German mobilization intensely from its inception. Then also, with the revival of the danger of war in the thirties, the antipatriotic pretense was completely dropped. Emphasis in Soviet propaganda fell less on world revolution and more on the glories of the Soviet Fatherland. A new Soviet nationalism, at once territorial and ideological, was now vigorously cultivated by the regime.

But the Communist movement outside the Soviet Union was also shaped by the overriding influence of the "national." The Soviets were the principal beneficiaries of the disillusion, alienation, and frustration wrought by the war. They inherited and revived the proletarian revolutionism that had foundered with the Second International in 1914. They also attempted to assume the leadership of the new movements of pacifism, internationalism, and (after the mid-thirties) antifascism, which were not particularly Marxist. At its core, however, communism outside the Soviet Union was a "substitute" nationalism. The Communist cult abroad was rooted in the conviction that it was in the Soviet Union that the ideals of these movements were best preached and practiced. "France is where we live," proclaimed an underground Communist pamphlet in 1940 before the fall of France, "but the Soviet Union is our fatherland." [7]

[7] A. Rossi, *Les Communistes français pendant la drôle de guerre* (Paris, 1951), p. 234.

To say that the Soviet regime or international communism was "nationalized," however, is not to say that either was identical with fascism, also compounded of the national and the social. Fascism was a war product peculiar to Europe outside the Soviet Union where communism was not strong enough to seize or hold power, but strong enough to produce panic in numerous elements. Movements of fascism arose almost simultaneously as competing revolutionary movements. Though fascism had prewar roots, the anti-Communist aspects of fascism were direct consequences of the war. The fear of proletarianization was particularly marked in a variety of social categories greatly enlarged by the war—clerical workers, government employees, pensioners, former officers, impoverished aristocrats, debt-ridden peasants. The same categories were likely to be outraged at Communist antipatriotism—what particularly rankled was the Communist argument that only capitalists had benefited from the war and that the slaughter had all been in vain. For these elements, the old terms of ideological debate were even less relevant than they had been before the war. The distinctions between right and left, bourgeois and proletarian, national and social did not give adequate expression to their needs. Fascist movements, characteristically, tended to combine at one time or another almost all the features of both right and left. Basically, fascist claims to nationalism were rooted in a concern for the national interest and tradition. Their claims to socialism lay in hostility to the individualism and particularism in capitalism, rather than to the profit system—fascism professed concern for the masses, the collectivity.

Fascist movements appeared virtually everywhere during the postwar era, but especially where communism threatened. In Italy Mussolini's movement, compounded of the national and social, progressively sacrificed the latter in the interests of the former. Once in power, the regime aimed at class collaboration and final resolution of the national-social antagonism. This role was assigned to the institutions of corporatism. These had been the subject of considerable prewar speculation by syndicalists and nationalists alike, but given greater relevance by the war experience with national socioeconomic management. In the Nazi movement, both before and after Hitler's accession to power, the social was also progressively sacrified in the interests of the national. National economic planning was introduced in 1936 with the beginning of war preparations. But if the Nazis favored management over labor, it was because they were guided more by productivity than by love of capitalism.

* * *

The war ended the ascendancy of European liberal democracy. This is not to say that the European world was completely "liberal" and "democratic" before 1914. Nor does this mean that liberal democratic goals had, in fact, been anywhere attained—only the states of western Europe approached them. But before the war, almost everywhere, the major currents of change had seemed to contemporaries to be working in the direction of these goals. After the war, even where the war had been won, this was no longer the case.

Even before the war there were signs of the weakening of liberal democracy. An insidious anti-intellectualism which received apparent support from the scientific and intellectual achievements of the age undermined the individualism, rationalism, and humanitarianism that underlay liberal conceptions. Particularly ominous was the appearance of revolutionary movements that cultivated, organized, and propagated beyond previous limits a variety of hatreds—class, nation or race hatred. *Raison d'état* progressively became the guiding light of statesmen and patriotism assumed a more and more aggressive and militaristic form. Even in the most favorable of national environments, where the apparatus of liberal democracy—civil liberties, universal manhood suffrage, party politics, parliamentary institutions, ministerial responsibility—was most solidly grounded, it sometimes failed to function. Liberal England could not avert suffragette, Irish, or labor violence. Republican France was shaken to its foundations during the Dreyfus Affair by the unsuspected depths of antisemitism. Still, on the eve of the first world conflict it is the persistence of liberal democracy that should be stressed, even where the "new liberalism" had created elements of the "welfare state." The vast majority of Europeans, certainly in the most advanced parts of Europe, believed in the efficacy of its methods and the desirability of its goals.

The war opened a new and difficult era for liberal democracy even where, it was asserted, the war was being fought in its name. The closing of ranks, such as the *Union sacrée* in France, freed governments from the criticism to which they were ordinarily subjected. They now made claims to authority that in peacetime would have entailed the risk of rebellion. By 1917 the concentration of power had taken on the character of government dictatorship. As the liberal bourgeoisie abdicated, the soldiers and organizers took over. Freedom of thought, which with few exceptions had been respected for half a century in Europe, went by the board. And yet, distinctions must be made. Although Britain was seriously threatened by the submarine menace and northeast France was under German occupation during the entire war, parliamentary institutions continued to function, however imperfectly, and no serious danger of military dictatorship arose. Clemenceau's quip that war was too important to be left to the generals was significant. In Germany the wartime mobilization not only emasculated the Reichstag and the civilian government generally, but culminated in a military dictatorship to which the Kaiser himself was obliged to submit. In Russia the liberal Provisional Government gave way to the Bolshevik dictatorship.

The postwar environment was not conducive to the successful operation of liberal democracy—the Soviet regime, moreover, was a disturbing innovation. And yet, 1919 appeared to be the high-water mark of liberal democracy. The victorious powers viewed the outcome of the war as confirmation of their own faith in democracy and eagerly sought to resume "normal" life. Self-determination and parliamentary government succeeded the multinational autocratic monarchies: The new regimes looked to parliamentary Britain or republican France for inspiration.

But all of democratic Europe found itself in serious difficulty in the immediate postwar years. The German republic—weakened by the unpopularity of Versailles and the pressure of domestic problems and threatened on all sides by extremist movements—was obliged to fight for its life. The Weimar regime, for the moment, survived, but Italian democracy did not. Though on the side of the victors, the conviction that the peace had been "lost" and the accumulated social distress aggravated by the war resulted in the breakdown of the parliamentary regime. In 1922 it fell victim to Mussolini's legions. Moreover, the lesser states, such as Hungary, Poland, and Yugoslavia, soon demonstrated little capacity to deal with postwar problems within a democratic framework. Still, in the twenties one could easily persuade oneself that neither the Soviet nor the Italian development was conclusive and that the problems of the newer states might also be temporary.

With the Great Depression, however, liberal democracy once again began to lose ground rapidly—by 1938 only ten of the twenty-seven countries of Europe retained something of the apparatus and spirit of democratic government. Even Britain and France fell into a quagmire. The methods of liberal democracy were too slow or too feeble and the difficulties were compounded by expanding extremist movements. That much of the liberal democratic tradition was saved was due to the employment of measures rather similar to those of the wartime emergency—"fronts" or coalition governments, high taxes and massive government intervention—and when necessary, rule by decree and banning of hostile organizations. What emerged here were the outlines of the "welfare state." But elsewhere in Europe the roots of democracy were planted in very shallow soil. There were no sizable groups that possessed a material interest in defending democratic institutions. The effects of the Depression, of the Nazi accession to power, and of the Anglo-French weakness were to undermine the basis of both internal and external stability. As experiments with democratic institutions failed, the new regimes turned to Italian Fascism or German Nazism for guidance. The democracies had won the war militarily; by 1939, they had lost it ideologically and institutionally.

* * *

The war greatly expanded and gave new vigor to movements with inclinations toward "total solutions." But not all such movements came to power and not all that came to power were able to establish totalitarian regimes. Totalitarianism was favored where an experiment with liberal parliamentary institutions had failed and where longstanding autocratic, military, and bureaucratic traditions survived—where the "welfare state" was ruled out, the "warfare state" got its chance.

The elements essential to totalitarianism already existed before the war, though in fragmented and disparate form. Indeed, in modern times, the tendency may be traced at least as far back as the French Revolution. The revolution had established concretely the notion of the social order as man-made, not imposed from above. The state of siege created by the Jacobins, moreover, introduced the idea of a revolutionary order totally mobilized to meet the dangers of war and counterrevolution—the Jacobin regime haunted nineteenth-century revolutionaries. By the end of the century, European institutions already bore the mark of the rise of the masses, of modern industry, and of the manipulation and management of both. These elements, however, were not yet combined nor were they anywhere at the disposal of a single authority. But totalitarian tendencies were more clearly in evidence in other quarters. The Bolshevik organization from its origins was in Lenin's conception, if not in reality, a miniature totalitarian system. Prewar movements such as revolutionary syndicalism in France and Italy, the *Action Française*, the Italian Nationalist party, the Austrian German Workers' party and the Pan-German League possessed, at the very least, a totalitarian rhetoric. They viewed the coming social order in essentially "totalist" and catastrophic terms. The old order was to be uprooted. Whatever could not be accommodated to the new order was in some manner to be liquidated.

Europeans were provided with their first taste of totalitarianism in total war. The new mobilization had required the combination of the prewar elements that already pointed in this direction. Nowhere, however, was the organization for war as comprehensive or as effective as in Germany where it was undoubtedly facilitated by the military tradition, though a major weakness lay in a propaganda disadvantage with respect to the Allies. The German experience was to have far-reaching consequences. Revolutionaries of all persuasions could see clearly for the first time the extraordinary energies that could be released in the modern social order and the almost unlimited powers at the command of the modern state. The first opportunity to employ the European but especially the German experience with total war came with the decomposition and dissolution of the Russian state. The collapse of the autocracy in 1917 left a void that could be filled only by a party prepared to employ extreme measures. What the Bolsheviks believed necessary to hold power was already implicit in the way in which they took it on November 7—the seizure of the power stations, telephone and telegraph exchanges, and railroad terminals. But to the extent that they used any model at all for maintaining power during the civil war and intervention, it was German *Kriegssozialismus*. "We must organize everything," wrote Lenin, "take everything into our hands. . . ." [8] The Bolsheviks appropriately labeled this period of the Soviet regime "War Communism." It foreshadowed the full totalitarian system that was to be introduced a decade later.

The war and its consequences furthered prewar totalitarian tendencies. In Russia the war, by favoring extremist and autocratic solutions, not only gave the Bolsheviks their chance, but determined in large part the character of the new regime. The collapse of 1917 had not only confirmed that of 1905, but also a long-standing conviction that Russia courted disaster when at war with more advanced powers. Since the time of Peter the Great there had been periodic efforts at reform and catching-up. But the coming of modern industry had only increased the gap. Lenin himself observed in September 1917, "War is inexorable and puts the question with unsparing sharpness: either perish or catch up and overtake the advanced countries." [9] Domestic chaos during the period of War Communism, however, did not permit the construction of an order of any permanence. Relaxation of the dictatorship was, in fact, necessary during the N.E.P. to stabilize

[8] Quoted in Theodore H. Von Laue, *Why Lenin? Why Stalin?* (New York, 1964), p. 157.

[9] *Ibid.*, p. 13.

the regime and to determine its future course. It was not until the introduction of the first Five-Year Plan in 1928 that the decisive step was taken. The wartime collapse and the danger of the renewal of war weighed heavily in the Soviet decision. Moreover, the war experience indicated how industrialization might be brought about. The problem the Soviets faced was not one of operating a working industrial system, but of creating one. It was in the name of industrialization that the totalitarian machine, the rudiments of which already existed, was perfected. Not the peacetime economies of the advanced countries, but the economy of total war—of rationing, of inflation, and of planning under centralized state control —was deemed appropriate. Also deemed essential was the exhilaration of battle, the *patrie-en-danger* psychosis, either real or contrived. The First Plan began with a "war scare," spy trials, and a program of military preparedness. In justification, Stalin in 1931 virtually repeated Lenin's argument of 1917:

> . . . those who lag behind are beaten. . . . We are fifty or a hundred years behind the advanced countries. We must make good this lag in ten years. Either we do it or they crush us.[10]

Once created, however, Soviet totalitarianism acquired a logic and momentum of its own. The virtual declaration of a state of siege, the mobilization of the masses at a high pitch of excitement required a continuing succession of "enemies." The periodic purge of "traitors" to the fatherland or to the proletariat effectively linked the foreign and domestic danger. Stalin stopped at no sacrifice. By 1939 only the United States and Germany outranked the Soviet Union in total industrial production. Herein lay the basis for both the Soviet triumph over Hitler and post-World War II bipolarization.

[10] Quoted in John L. Snell, *Illusion and Necessity: the Diplomacy of Global War, 1939–1945* (Boston, 1963), p. 22.

As for Italian Fascism, it was to establish the decor of totalitarianism outside the Soviet Union, but it never became a rigorous system. The postwar crisis in Italy was not as grave as the German one and abated by itself. Even after Hitler's prompting in 1938, the Italian regime lacked the ruthlessness of the Soviets or Nazis. In the lesser states, from the Baltic to the Adriatic and Black seas, pseudototalitarian systems emerged by the late thirties. These derived partly from the war experience and partly in imitation of or because of pressure by Italy or Germany. But these regimes—royal, military or political dictatorships—were based largely on police measures and possessed neither substantial ideological foundation nor mass support.

Nazi totalitarianism, as well as Soviet, was a direct descendant of the war. The German breakdown, though not as precipitous as the Russian, also began during the war. The imperial government gave way to a military dictatorship in 1917 and the monarchy collapsed in 1918. But the breakdown continued after the war with the middle-class debacle in the inflation of 1923 and the collapse of the parliamentary republic in 1931–32. Both the French occupation of the Ruhr that led to the inflation and the Depression that reduced the Weimar government to impotence brought home to Germans the *fact* of defeat which the events of October, 1918 had somehow failed to do. It was the Ruhr crisis, moreover, that brought the Nazis to national prominence and the Depression that brought them to power. Few Germans had been tempted by Hitler until the Depression revived the anxieties and fears produced by the defeat of 1918.

The Nazi movement, however, was not only a product of the breakdown produced by the war, it was itself rooted conceptually in the war experience. Hitler in *Mein Kampf* and even in his "conversations" during the Second World

War was constantly preoccupied with German defeat in the first. The mobilization of 1917–18 had not gone far enough—if only he had been at the helm. "If I'd been Reich Chancellor . . . I'd have cut the throat of all obstruction. . . ." [11] Nazi writers were especially struck by Ludendorff's critique of the German domestic scene during the war and his proposal for an "armed state" without politics, prepared to conduct a future total war. What the Nazis aimed at was a militarized pan-Germanism, a regime that bore none of the weaknesses of the wartime mobilization. But their concern was with the permanent organization of the nation, in peace and in war. Totalitarianism was not a means to an end; it was the end itself. The need for rapid industrialization, as in the Soviet case, did not exist. Germany already possessed the most modern industrial plant in Europe. The *Gleichschaltung* (bringing-into-line) placed under general party influence or direction all phases of national life, though drastic change was not everywhere required. The totalitarian features of the new regime were most pronounced, however, in the radically new conception of the nation as a biological entity engaged in a struggle for survival. Whether or not Nazi leaders believed in the race doctrine is irrelevant. What is relevant is the purpose the doctrine was to serve. For the Nazis, both domestic and international politics was warfare. For German "national socialism," the Jewish "race" could be effectively depicted as the enemy—Communist or capitalist, domestic or foreign.

* * *

In sum, the problem of the First World War as turning point would appear to be basic to the meaning of contemporary history. With the spotlight on the events of

[11] Quoted in H. R. Trevor-Roper, ed., *Hitler's Secret Conversations, 1941–1944* (New York, 1961), p. 43.

1914–18, both the prewar and postwar worlds are illuminated. Although the illumination is necessarily selective, what emerges are the very outlines of our time.

What were the roots of the turning point? Some historians have argued that it is in the Renaissance and particularly in the rise of secularism that the origins of the twentieth-century cataclysms are to be found. While necessarily tentative, this kind of speculation can be instructive, for it points to a possible relation of the war to deeper tendencies and to something of the quality of the transformation itself. It is, however, from the era of the French Revolution and the Industrial Revolution that the unmistakable signs of our time appear. They are to be found in the claim of the masses to political power, in the rise of modern industry, and in the emerging techniques of managing the social and material order. These grew rapidly in importance in the nineteenth century and became irresistible and revolutionary in the twentieth. From the final quarter of the nineteenth century, however, the currents that have shaped our time came into focus, at times tentative in aspect or only vaguely suspected. Some crystallized in and were given direction by spectacular events: the unification of Germany, the Franco-Russian Alliance, the Boxer Rebellion, the Spanish-American War, the Russo-Japanese War, the July Crisis. Others worked themselves out in the new science, scholarship and art, the depression of 1873 and the effects of economic exposure generally, and the new political and social ferment. There were no air-tight compartments in this development. International affairs had domestic consequences; scientific, philosophical, or artistic movements had political consequences. And the reverse was also true. But in retrospect, by 1914 these tendencies, at least in their general character, were not to be denied. If the war had come sooner or if it had come later, if the war had been limited or if there had been no war but a peaceful evolution, the tendencies would have been there. One way or another, the new military potential, the transformation of the European balance, the rise of anticolonialism, as well as the intellectual revolt, the transformation of capitalism, and the challenge to liberal democracy would have undoubtedly imposed themselves on any development regardless of its general character.

As for the nature of the turning point, the war placed these prewar tendencies on the center of the historical stage, put its own stamp on them, and passed them on to the future. The effect of the war was to influence not only their strength but their character. What had been an idea before the war now became a hard reality. What had been characteristic of a minority was provided with a mass basis. What had been an inclination became a conscious purpose. But the reverse was also true. By upsetting prewar relations, the war made for fluidity of conditions—it accelerated or slowed, favored or resisted. That the impress of the war was so deep was due to its intensity, its global scope, and its duration. The war was no mere interruption, no "parenthesis," in the "normal" course of history, as the limited and frequently longer wars of the eighteenth century tended to be. The war was a truly revolutionary experience. 1789 had begun with revolution and ended with war; 1914 began with war and ended in revolution. As a catastrophic occurrence, therefore, the war imposed its own character on the transformation already under way. If not for the war, the pre-1914 tendencies might have worked themselves out differently. The war thus gave to the transformation an "accidental" quality. And the war was now to transmit its creation to the postwar era. It did so by its immediate results, by the conditions and problems it left in its wake, and by the convictions it engendered—by the "lessons" it appeared to teach about the past, the present, and the future prospects of mankind.

What were the consequences of the turning point? The

major developments of the interwar period, beginning with Versailles, were, at the very least, war-related if not war-dominated: the postwar economic difficulties, the disillusionment, the rise of communism and fascism, the crash of 1929 and the Great Depression, the Manchurian War, the totalitarianism of the thirties, the destruction of the Versailles system, the outbreak of war in 1939, and in broad outline, even the Second World War. All were part of the same development, all had their roots in the First World War. But the "persistence" of the war long after the official cease fire only points to its inconclusive character. The war had failed to make a clean sweep—that is why contemporaries so little understood its consequences. The war had resulted in a blurring of distinctions which in an earlier framework had been reasonably clearcut: warfare and diplomacy, war and peace, military and civilian, international and domestic, politics and economics, nationalism and socialism. Few could see or even wanted to see clearly. The interwar era, consequently, was one of monumental blunders and even more monstrous crimes. It was marked by endemic civil war within each nation and within the international community generally. In effect, what the Second World War did was to sweep away much of the unfinished business of the first, thereby clarifying its meaning. The second war confirmed the rise of total war and the advent of the new diplomacy, the end of the European balance and the triumph of the superpowers, the revolt against Europe and the rise of global history: For Europe this meant political division and incorporation (more or less) into the orbits, both international and domestic, of either the United States or the Soviet Union. Moreover, the mobilization of 1939–45 may very well have completed the work of the mobilization of 1914–18. In a sense, the bomb dropped on Hiroshima may be regarded as the final product of the two mobilizations. The mobilization of the first war, therefore, which so dominated the interwar years, may have contained the seeds of its own negation. The atomic warfare introduced in the final moments of World War II could conceivably no longer require a future wartime mobilization—massive and instantaneous atomic warfare may have rendered obsolete the most unique creation of the First World War.

Viewed in this light, the role of the First World War as turning point assumes a double significance—it was a turning point not only for modern history, but possibly, for all history. The war accelerated and combined the burgeoning revolutionary forces of the nineteenth century, and imposed its stamp—at once catastrophic and global—on them, to shape thereby the destinies of the twentieth century. But it also broke two barriers never before overcome in human history—the barrier of scarcity and the possible elimination of poverty and the barrier of destruction and the possible annihilation of humanity. The breakdown, begun in the mobilization of the first war, reached its climax in the mobilization of the second. The collapse of these barriers leads to a future as yet unknown.

SUGGESTED READINGS

Albrecht-Carrié, René. *The Meaning of the First World War*. Englewood Cliffs, N.J., 1965.

Arendt, Hannah. *On Revolution*. New York, 1963.

———. *The Origins of Totalitarianism*. New York, 1960.

Aron, Raymond. *The Century of Total War*. Boston, 1955.

Bailey, Thomas A. *Woodrow Wilson and the Great Betrayal*. New York, 1945.

———. *Woodrow Wilson and the Lost Peace*. New York, 1944.

Borsody, Stephen. *The Tragedy of Central Europe*. New York, 1962.

Carr, Edward H. *International Relations Between Two World Wars, 1919–1939*. London, 1963.

———. *The Twenty Years' Crisis*. New York, 1956.

———. *The New Society*. Boston, 1951.

Chambers, Frank P. *The War Behind the War: A History of the Political and Civilian Fronts*. New York, 1939.

Churchill, Winston S. *The World Crisis: the Aftermath*. London, 1929.

Craig, Gordon A. *From Bismarck to Adenauer*. New York, 1965.

———. *The Politics of the Prussian Army, 1640–1945*. Oxford, Eng., 1955.

———, and Felix Gilbert, eds. *The Diplomats, 1919–1939*. Princeton, N.J., 1953.

Cruttwell, C. R. M. F. *A History of the Great War, 1914–1918*, 2nd ed. London, 1936.

Dean, Vera M. *Europe and the United States*. New York, 1950.

Earle, Edward M., ed. *Makers of Modern Strategy*. New York, 1966.

Erlich, Alexander. *The Soviet Industrialization Debate, 1924–1928.* Cambridge, Mass., 1950.
Friedrich, Carl J., and Zbigniew K. Brzezinski. *Totalitarian Dictatorship and Autocracy.* New York, 1965.
Halévy, Elie. *The Era of Tyrannies,* translated by R. K. Webb. New York, 1965.
Hancock, W. K. *Four Studies of War and Peace in this Century.* Cambridge, Eng., 1961.
Hayes, Carlton J. H. *A Generation of Materialism, 1871–1900.* New York, 1963.
Hoffman, Stanley. *The State of War.* New York, 1965.
Holborn, Hajo. *The Political Collapse of Europe.* New York, 1951.
Hughes, H. Stuart. *Consciousness and Society.* New York, 1961.
"International Fascism, 1920–1945," *Journal of Contemporary History,* I (1966), 1–197.
Joll, James. *Three Intellectuals in Politics: Blum, Rathenau, Marinetti.* New York, 1965.
Kennan, George F. *Russia and the West Under Lenin and Stalin.* New York, 1962.
———. *Russia, the Atom and the West.* New York, 1958.
———. *American Diplomacy, 1900–1950.* Chicago, 1951.
Keynes, John M. *The Economic Consequences of the Peace.* New York, 1920.
Lafore, Laurence. *The Long Fuse: An Interpretation of the Origins of World War I.* New York, 1965.
Langer, William L. *The Diplomacy of Imperialism, 1890–1902.* New York, 1951.
———. *European Alliances and Alignments, 1871–1890.* New York, 1950.
Masur, Gerhard. *Prophets of Yesterday.* New York, 1961.
May, Ernest R. *The World War and American Isolation, 1914–1917.* Cambridge, Mass., 1959.
Mayer, Arno J. *Wilson vs. Lenin: Political Origins of the New Diplomacy, 1917–1918.* New York, 1964.
Mendelssohn-Bartholdy, A. *The War and German Society.* New Haven, Conn., 1937.
Mumford, Lewis. *Techniques and Civilization.* New York, 1963.
Namier, Lewis B. *Vanished Supremacies.* New York, 1963.
———. *Europe in Decay: A Study in Disintegration, 1936–1940.* London, 1950.
———. *Diplomatic Prelude, 1938–1939.* London, 1948.
Nicolson, Harold. *Peacemaking, 1919.* New York, 1965.

"1914," *Journal of Contemporary History*, I (1966), 3–210.
Nolte, Ernst. *Three Faces of Fascism*, translated by Leila Vennewitz. New York, 1966.
Rogger, Hans, and Eugene Weber, eds. *The European Right: A Historical Profile*. Berkeley, Calif., 1965.
Ropp, Theodore. *War in the Modern World*. Durham, N.C., 1959.
Schmitt, Bernadotte E. *The Coming of the War: 1914*. New York, 1930.
Seaman, L. C. B. *From Vienna to Versailles*. London, 1955.
Shapiro, Leonard. *The Communist Party of the Soviet Union*. New York, 1960.
Smith, Daniel M. *The Great Departure: The United States and World War I*. New York, 1965.
Snell, John L. *Illusion and Necessity: The Diplomacy of Global War, 1939–1945*. Boston, 1963.
Stolper, Gustav. *The German Economy, 1870 to the Present*. New York, 1967.
Taylor, A. J. P. *The Origins of the Second World War*. New York, 1961.
Trevor-Roper, H. R., ed. *Hitler's Secret Conversations, 1941–1944*. New York, 1961.
Tuchman, Barbara. *The Proud Tower*. New York, 1966.
———. *The Guns of August*. New York, 1962.
Von Laue, Theodore. *Why Lenin? Why Stalin?* New York, 1964.
Weber, Eugene. *Varieties of Fascism*. New York, 1964.
Weinberg, Gerhard L. *Germany and the Soviet Union, 1939–1941*. Leiden, 1954.
Wheeler-Bennett, John W. *The Nemesis of Power: The German Army in Politics, 1918–1945*. London, 1953.
———. *Munich: Prologue to Tragedy*. New York, 1948.
———. *The Forgotten Peace: Brest-Litovsk*. London, 1938.
Wolfers, Arnold. *Britain and France Between Two Wars*. New York, 1940.

INDEX

About the Authors

Gordon A. Craig, who holds advanced degrees from Princeton and Oxford Universities, is a specialist in European history, particularly in its military and diplomatic aspects. His books include *The Politics of the Prussian Army, 1940–1945, From Bismarck to Adenauer: Aspects of German Statecraft, The Battle of Königgrätz* and, most recently, *War, Politics and Diplomacy.* Professor of History at Stanford University and Honorary Professor of the Free University of Berlin, Dr. Craig is a member of the American Philosophical Society and the American Academy of Arts and Sciences.

Carl J. Friedrich is Eaton Professor of the Science of Government at Harvard, where he has been a member of the faculty since 1926. He was Professor of Political Science (now Emeritus) at the University of Heidelberg and Director of its *Institut für Politische Wissenschaft* from 1956 to 1966. The holder of many honorary degrees, Professor Friedrich is a Vice President of the International Political Science Association and a past President of the American Political Science Association. Among his books are *Man and His Government, Constitutional Government and Democracy, Totalitarian Dictatorship and Autocracy* (with Z. Brzezinski), *The Philosophy of Law in Historical Perspective,* and *The Age of the Baroque.*

Charles Hirschfeld received his Ph.D. from Johns Hopkins University in 1939, and, after wartime service in the Pacific, joined the faculty of Michigan State University, where he is now Professor of History in Justin Morrill College. He has served as a Fulbright lecturer in American Studies in Italy and is the recipient of a 1966 Distinguished Faculty Award from Michigan State University. Professor Hirschfeld is the author of *Baltimore 1870–1900: Studies in Social History, The Great Railroad Conspiracy: The Social History of a Railroad War, Classics of Western Thought: The Modern World,* and, most recently, articles on "Nationalist Progressivism and World War I," and "Brooks Adams and American Nationalism."

Hans Kohn, now Professor Emeritus of History of The City University of New York, is the holder of several honorary degrees in addition to that of Doctor Juris, 1923, from the German University of his native Prague. A Guggenheim Fellow in 1940, he was also a Fellow of the Institute of Advanced Studies at Princeton, 1948, 1955, and of the Center of Advanced Study at Middletown, Connecticut, 1963–1964. Professor Kohn's concern with the history of ideas is reflected in his works, among which are *Martin Buber, seine Zeit und sein Werk, The Idea of Nationalism, Pan-Slavism, Its History and Ideology*, and *The German Mind.*

Jack J. Roth, Professor and Chairman of the History Department of Roosevelt University, received his training at the University of Chicago and at the *Institut d'études politiques* (University of Paris). A specialist in modern European intellectual history, Professor Roth is co-translator of *Georges Sorel, Reflections on Violence,* and has published articles and reviews in many scholarly journals, the most recent being "The Roots of Italian Fascism: Sorel and Sorelismo" (*Journal of Modern History,* March 1967).

A Note on the Type

The text of this book is set in Electra, a typeface designed by W(illiam) A(ddison) Dwiggins for the Mergenthaler Linotype Company and first made available in 1935. Electra cannot be classified as either "modern" or "old style." In general, it is a simple, readable typeface which attempts to give a feeling of fluidity, power, and speed.

W. A. *Dwiggins* (1880–1956) began an association with the Mergenthaler Linotype Company in 1929, and over the next twenty-seven years designed a number of book types, of which Metro, Electra, and Caledonia have been used very widely.

Composed, printed, and bound by The Colonial Press Inc., Clinton, Mass. Typography by Leon Bolognese.